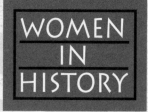

WOMEN
IN
HISTORY

Women of Colonial America

Lydia Bjornlund

LUCENT
BOOKS®

THOMSON

★

GALE

San Diego • Detroit • New York • San Francisco • Cleveland • New Haven, Conn. • Waterville, Maine • London • Munich

THOMSON

GALE

On cover: Elizabeth Paddy Wensley, one of America's strong and
resourceful colonial women, sat for this portrait in the 1670s.

LIBRARY OF CONGRESS CATALOGING-IN-PUBLICATION DATA

Bjornlund, Lydia
  Women of colonial America / by Lydia Bjornlund.
    v. cm. — (Women in history series)
  Includes bibliographical references and index.
  Summary: Discusses the place of colonial women in the home, the workplace, in
  Native American communities, and as slaves and servants. The women are also
  examined in their roles as activists and leaders in the church and the community.
  Contents: Settling in the New World—Women in Native American communities—
  Colonial women in the home and family—Servants and slaves—Women in the
  workforce—Church and community leaders—Taking a stand: colonial women as
  political activists.
    ISBN 1-59018-470-X (hardback : alk. paper)
  1. Women—United States—History. 2. Women colonists—United States—Social
  conditions. 3. Women colonists—United States—Economic conditions. 4. Indian
  women—United States—History. 5. Women slaves—United States—History.
  6. Indentured servants—United States—History. 7. United States—History—
  Colonial period, ca. 1600–1775. [1. Women—United States—History—17th century.
  2. Women—United States—History—18th century. 3. Colonists. 4. Indian women—
  History. 5. Slaves. 6. Indentured servants. 7. United States—History—Colonial
  period, ca. 1600–1775.] I. Title. II. Women in history (San Diego, Calif.)
    HQ1416.B5 2004
    305.4'0973—dc21
                                                                        2003010396

Printed in the United States of America

Contents

❦

Foreword   4

Introduction: Settling in the New World   6

Chapter 1:
Women in Native American Communities   8

Chapter 2:
Colonial Women in the Home and Family   24

Chapter 3:
Servants and Slaves   37

Chapter 4:
Colonial Women in the Workforce   53

Chapter 5:
Church and Community Leaders   67

Chapter 6:
Taking a Stand: Colonial Women as Political Activists   80

Notes   95
For Further Reading   100
Works Consulted   103
Index   107
Picture Credits   112
About the Author   112

Foreword

The story of the past as told in traditional historical writings all too often leaves the impression that if men are not the only actors in the narrative, they are assuredly the main characters. With a few notable exceptions, males were the political, military, and economic leaders in virtually every culture throughout recorded time. Since traditional historical scholarship focuses on the public arenas of government, foreign relations, and commerce, the actions and ideas of men—or at least of powerful men—are naturally at the center of conventional accounts of the past.

In the last several decades, however, many historians have abandoned their predecessors' emphasis on "great men" to explore the past "from the bottom up," a phenomenon that has had important consequences for the study of women's history. These social historians, as they are known, focus on the day-to-day experiences of the "silent majority"—those people typically omitted from conventional scholarship because they held relatively little political or economic sway within their societies. In the new social history, members of ethnic and racial minorities, factory workers, peasants, slaves, children, and women are no longer relegated to the background but are placed at the very heart of the narrative.

Around the same time social historians began broadening their research to include women and other previously neglected elements of society, the feminist movement of the late 1960s and 1970s was also bringing unprecedented attention to the female heritage. Feminists hoped that by examining women's past experiences, contemporary women could better understand why and how gender-based expectations had developed in their societies, as well as how they might reshape inherited—and typically restrictive—economic, social, and political roles in the future.

Today, some four decades after the feminist and social history movements gave new impetus to the study of women's history, there is a rich and continually growing body of work on all aspects of women's lives in the past. The Lucent Books Women in History series draws upon this abundant and diverse literature to introduce students to women's experiences within a variety of past cultures and time periods in terms of the distinct roles they filled. In their capacities as workers, activists, and artists, women exerted significant influence on important events whether they conformed to or broke from traditional roles. The Women in History titles depict extraordinary women who managed to attain positions of influence in their male-dominated societies, including such celebrated heroines as the feisty medieval queen Eleanor of Aquitaine, the brilliant propagandist of the American Revolution Mercy Otis Warren, and the courageous African American activist of the Civil War era Harriet Tubman. Included as well are the stories of the ordinary—and often overlooked—women of the past who also helped shape their societies myriad ways—moral, intellectual, and economic—without straying far from customary gender roles: the housewives and mothers, school teachers and church volunteers, midwives and nurses and wartime camp followers.

In this series, readers will discover that many of these unsung women took more significant parts in the great political and social upheavals of their day than has often been recognized. In *Women of the American Revolution,* for example, students will learn how American housewives assumed a crucial role in helping the Patriots win the war against Britain. They accomplished this by planting and harvesting fields, producing and trading goods, and doing whatever else was necessary to maintain the family farm or business in the absence of their soldier husbands despite the heavy burden of housekeeping and child-care duties they already bore. By their self-sacrificing actions, competence, and ingenuity, these anonymous heroines not only kept their families alive, but kept the economy of their struggling young nation going as well during eight long years of war.

Each volume in this series contains generous commentary from the works of respected contemporary scholars, but the Women in History series particularly emphasizes quotations from primary sources such as diaries, letters, and journals whenever possible to allow the women of the past to speak for themselves. These firsthand accounts not only help students to better understand the dimensions of women's daily spheres—the work they did, the organizations they belonged to, the physical hardships they faced—but also how they viewed themselves and their actions in the light of their society's expectations for their sex.

The distinguished American historian Mary Beard once wrote that women have always been a "force in history." It is hoped that the books in this series will help students to better appreciate the vital yet often little-known ways in which women of the past have shaped their societies and cultures.

Introduction:
Settling in the New World

The women of colonial America, the period beginning with the founding of Jamestown in 1607 and ending with the American Revolution of 1776, lived under the same conventions and restrictions that had governed their lives in Europe. Most of the American colonies followed English customs and laws, which allowed women few rights. Married women suffered what was known as "civil death," a state of affairs in which women had few individual rights. Women were not allowed to vote or to bring suit in a court of law. Any money that a married woman inherited or earned was under her husband's control. Before 1840 a Massachusetts law even prohibited a woman from spending money without the explicit approval of her husband, father, or other male guardian.

Although the legal system of the colonies mirrored that of England, the different circumstances in which women found themselves led to vastly different cultural norms. In Europe, a woman working out of doors was frowned upon; such work was considered a man's work. But the women who traveled across the Atlantic Ocean could not afford to abide by such customs. Their very survival depended on their ability to help find food. The women

Women of colonial America lived under the same conventions and restrictions as women in Europe.

who helped settle Massachusetts Bay, for example, dug for mussels and clams to support their diet. Women settling the frontier helped build houses and foraged the nearby woods for nuts and berries. And women throughout the colonies helped their husbands in the fields and tended small gardens near their houses. Of course, women assumed these tasks in addition to their customary domestic responsibilities; colonial housewives ran the household, cooked and cleaned, and made the family's clothing, soap, and candles.

As the colonies gained wealth, the tasks of the colonial Americans—women as well as men—became more diverse. Widows and the few women who remained single eked out a living using whatever property and skills they had at their disposal. They became innkeepers, artisans, printers, and merchants. Married women also toiled in a variety of ways to supplement their husbands' income. The wives of artisans often had shops where they sold their husbands' wares. Other housewives took children into their homes in so-called dame schools. Women of property managed complex households that often included indentured servants and slaves—an inexpensive but volatile workforce on which the economy of the South became increasingly dependent.

Women also gained stature in their churches and communities, often working in informal networks, but their influence varied. Governing bodies in some small communities sought the opinions of independent-minded women before making decisions; in other places, women who spoke their minds were perceived as a threat to the established order. As anti-British sentiment grew during the 1760s and 1770s, women found their collective voice, organizing boycotts of British goods and joining together to use their power as the purchasers and users of domestic goods as a weapon.

The women of colonial America faced many obstacles to becoming leaders in business, the church, or the community. The education of most girls focused almost exclusively on teaching the skills they needed as a housewife. Colonial laws and customs encouraged docility and obedience, and scorned independent thinking among women. Yet, an impressive number of women succeeded in finding their own way, becoming wealthy, independent women.

But it is not only these few shining examples of womanhood that are to be remembered. Countless women whose names have been forgotten worked hard to shape their society. Throughout the colonial era and throughout the colonies, women played a critical role in the success of their families, the American colonies, and American independence. These are the lives of the colonial women who established a new home, a new community, and a new nation out of the wilderness.

Chapter 1:
Women in Native American Communities

❧

The lands bounded by the Atlantic coast and the Mississippi River were the first regions of North America settled by Europeans. Long before these Europeans came, the lands were occupied by a host of Native American nations and tribes. The nations varied greatly in size, structure, and culture. All would be changed by the encroachment of European settlements.

Native Americans played a key role in supporting the fledgling settlements along the Atlantic coast in the early seventeenth century. The natives who lived nearby taught the colonists critical survival skills. Among the most important of these skills were those practiced by women: sowing and harvesting corn, squash, pumpkins, and other native foods; catching and cooking the shellfish that were plentiful along the Atlantic coastline; and cultivating and mixing herbs for medicinal purposes.

In fact, the first European settlements might not have survived had the colonists not had good neighbors. But in addition to trading partnerships and marriages with Native Americans, there was conflict and war. Throughout the colonial era, the worlds of the white settlers and their Native American neighbors coexisted and cooperated, clashed and collided.

Women's Work

The Native Americans followed age-old traditions. In a broad sense, work was divided between the sexes, with men taking on the roles of hunting and fishing, fighting battles with neighboring tribes, and protecting their turf. Women focused on home and family, which entailed a broad range of responsibilities from raising children to gathering and preparing food to tending the crops to making the clothes.

In practice, however, the division of labor was not clear cut. Native American men caught the fish, but women cleaned and cooked them. Men hunted and trapped animals, but women cooked and cured them. Men tanned the animal hides, but women made them into clothing. Men procured the poles and bark for their living quarters; women used those materials to construct shelter from cold, rain, and snow.

Women traveled with men as they hunted for game, searched for a new site to plant crops or build a home, or convened with neighbors to discuss regional issues or hammer out differences. Although women did not usually engage in such endeavors, they played a critical role. One Chipewyan guide wrote, "Women . . . pitch our tents, make and mend our clothing, keep us warm at night; and, in fact, there is no such thing as traveling any considerable distance, or for any length of time, in this country, without their assistance."[1]

In agricultural tribes, women also were responsible for growing the crops. Algonquian and Iroquois women tended large family plots, cultivating corn, beans, squash, and pumpkins as the staple crops. To supplement this diet, women gathered nuts, berries, and maple sap from the nearby forests. In some tribes, the work of women

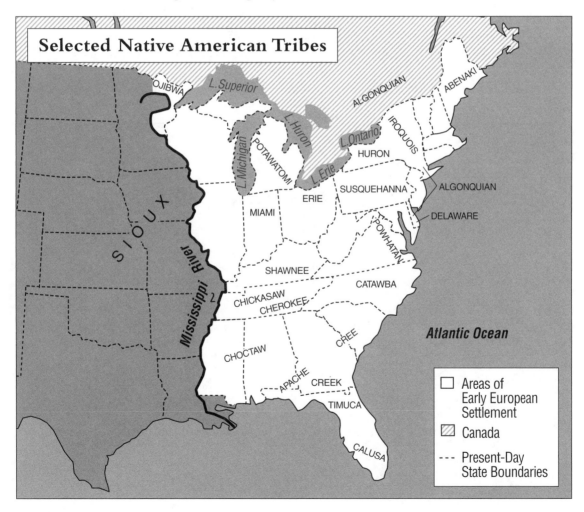

Selected Native American Tribes

Areas of Early European Settlement

Canada

- - - Present-Day State Boundaries

accounted for over 80 percent of the food supply.

Native American women also made a range of everyday household items, such as cooking and eating utensils, storage pits, benches, mats, wooden racks, and the like. In more nomadic hunting and herding groups, which moved on a seasonal basis, women often were responsible for dismantling shelters, transporting household goods to the next location, and pitching the tribe's new homes.

Native American women in the Great Lakes region also played an important role in the fur trade. Among many Native American groups, women traveled with the fur trappers carrying the furs from place to place. They might also trap small animals themselves and sell their pelts. Even in communities in which women stayed behind in the village, it was women who helped prepare the furs to trade for European goods.

Most Native American groups accepted some role reversal, particularly women who took on more "masculine" roles. It was not unusual for women to serve as traders, scouts, hunters, warriors, or even

A group of Indian women leaves the village to hunt. In many Native American tribes, women served as hunters, scouts, and warriors.

Women of Colonial America

chiefs (female chiefs were often called queens). In some nations, the eldest child (male or female) of the eldest sister of the chief took over his position; in others, a daughter succeeded the chief if he had no male descendants.

Early colonists viewed the division of labor among native men and women as unbalanced. Samuel de Champlain, the famed French explorer who traveled throughout northern North America, thought the native people he encountered there treated their women little better than mules. Huron women, he reported, "have almost the whole care of the house and the work." It was women who "till the soil, sow the Indian corn, fetch wood for the winter,"; it was women who "strip the hemp, and spin it."[2] Similarly, in 1651, Edward Johnson wrote in a history of New England that Native American women "are generally very laborious at their planting time, and the men extraordinarily idle, making their squaws to carry their children and the luggage beside; so that many times they travel eight or ten miles with a burden on their backs, more fitter for a horse to carry than a woman. The men follow no kind of labor but hunting, fishing, and fowling."[3]

Yet most women did not seem to think that their share of the work was unduly strenuous. Mary Jemison, a white woman, was captured and adopted by the Seneca as a child in 1758. In a famous example of a literary genre of the era called captivity narratives, she wrote:

Our labor was not severe. Notwithstanding the Indian women have all the fuel and bread to procure, their task is probably not harder than that of white women, who have those articles provided for them; and their cares certainly are not half as numerous, nor as great. In the summer season, we planted, tended, and harvested our corn, and generally had all of our children with us; but had no master to oversee or drive us, so that we could work as leisurely as we pleased.[4]

Organization and Governance

According to what is known as a matrilineal system, many Native American nations traced their lineage on their mother's side of the family. When a man married, he became part of his wife's family. A new husband moved into his wife's abode, where he might live with her parents and other members of her extended family. In many tribes, if the couple could not manage a successful union, the wife initiated divorce proceedings simply by placing her husband's possessions outside the door of the dwelling. Usually, any children remained with their mother.

Even in nations that were not strictly matrilineal, women played a critical role in the organization of the community. For example, while membership in the clan of the Chippewa was inherited through the father, domestic life was organized through the bloodline of the mother. The important events of everyday life were controlled by hunting bands made up of matrilineal family units who lived next door to each other in individual wigwams belonging to the wife.

Perhaps the nation group in which women played the most powerful role was the Iroquois. Joseph-François Lafitau, a Jesuit missionary, wrote of the power of Iroquois women in 1724:

> There is nothing more real than this superiority of the women. . . . All real authority is vested in them. The land, the fields, and their harvest all belong to them. They are the souls of the councils, the arbiters of peace and of war. They have charge of the public treasury. To them are given the slaves. They arrange marriages. The children are their domain, and it is through their blood that the order of succession is transmitted.[5]

The organization of Iroquois villages supported the political role played by women. The Iroquois lived in large structures called longhouses. Each longhouse was shared by several families related through their mother. The oldest and most respected woman of the longhouse presided over its governance and its ceremonies.

Iroquois women also played a role in the politics of the village. Although men typically were chiefs and held other positions of power, Iroquois women also played an important advisory role. One French missionary observed that Iroquois women "were always the first to deliberate on private and community matters. They hold their councils apart and, as a result of their decisions, advise the chiefs."[6] Clan mothers nominated the leaders of the village and could remove them from office. Another French missionary wrote, "They did not hesitate, when the occasion required, to 'knock off the horns,' as it was technically called, from the head of a chief and send him back to the ranks of the warriors."[7]

In addition to making important decisions about community leadership, women oversaw the community's stock of corn, meal, and other grains; fresh, dried, and smoked meats; furs and animal pelts; and strings and belts of wampum, the Native American currency. The family's agricultural fields, tools, and other personal property were passed down through the mother.

Women played a political role in other nations as well. The women of the Ojibwa, for example, were in charge of deciding how food—including the deer and other game men brought back from a hunt—would be distributed. In the Cree and Cherokee nations, women who achieved the high status of Beloved Woman had

Women of Colonial America

The Iroquois lived in longhouses like these. The oldest and most respected woman of the family ran the affairs of each house.

final say about the fate of prisoners and could veto decisions to go to war.

Alliance Through Marriage

The first European explorers and traders counted Native American women among their scouts and translators. Women also proved to be a valuable tool for sealing an alliance through marriage. The Native Americans had for many generations arranged marriages to forge alliances with other villages and tribes; now, they did so with the powerful whites they encountered. Cree chiefs and leaders, for example, often reserved at least one of their daughters to offer as a wife to the traders who did business with them.

The most well known example of this practice involved Pocahontas. Although the story of Pocahontas is usually filled with romance, many historians believe that her marriage to John Rolfe was part of an effort to forge an alliance between her tribe and the English colonists. The daughter of Chief Powhatan, a powerful Algonquian leader, Pocahontas was just a teenager when she first met John Smith and the group of men who settled in Jamestown, Virginia. Pocahontas was curious about these strangers and spent time trading and talking among them. She taught them to communicate in her language, and she learned bits of English.

According to legend, when the Algonquian tribe sentenced John Smith to death, Pocahontas entreated her father to stop the execution. Historians question Smith's account of the event in which Pocahontas threw herself on him as the ax was about to fall, but they generally agree that

The Legend of Pocahontas

Pocahontas is perhaps the most famous of the Native American women who interacted with the early European settlers. The daughter of Chief Powhatan, a powerful Algonquian leader, Pocahontas was just a teenager when she first met John Smith and the group of men who settled in Jamestown, Virginia. In *The Colonial Mosaic: American Women, 1600–1760,* historian Jane Kamensky describes what happened to Pocahontas after she saved the life of John Smith:

From 1607 on, Pocahontas would live between two cultures, one English and one—as Smith's people mistakenly called it—"Indian." Among the colonizers and with her father's people she would continue to serve as a translator of English and Algonquian worlds. She would also become an important bridge between these two groups, promoting mutual understanding between English and Algonquian worlds. She would help the strangers to flourish in her land. And, at the same time, she would help her people resist annihilation at the strangers' hands.

In April 1563, . . . Virginia's leaders abducted Pocahontas and held her hostage in an attempt to gain a better bargaining position in negotiations with her father. During the long months of imprisonment, Pocahontas renounced the religious traditions of her birth and was christened as a member of the Church of England. Formally baptized into English culture, she took a new English name: Rebecca. She would soon also take an English husband. In April 1614, only days after her release, she married John Rolfe, an English tobacco planter whom she met during her captivity.

Though they might have celebrated her transformation from Indian princess to Christian woman, her adopted English family was never unaware of her foreignness. . . . It . . . seems sadly fitting that the unfamiliar damp cold of London soon proved ruinous to her health. . . . Bound at last for her native Werowocomoco (her husband's Virginia) in March 1617, she died of pneumonia or tuberculosis before the ship left the harbor.

Pocahontas succeeded in persuading her father to spare Smith's life. In doing so, Jane Kamensky concludes, Pocahontas "changed the course of American history [and] likely prevented the struggling settlement at Jamestown from suffering the fate of Roanoke, the 'lost' English colony that had vanished in 1591."[8] It was perhaps in an effort to reaffirm and strengthen the bonds between two communities that Powhatan arranged for the marriage of his daughter to wealthy tobacco owner John Rolfe in 1614.

Such marriages between white settlers and Native Americans occurred throughout the colonies, especially in places where there was a shortage of white women. European fur traders (first the French, and later Dutch and English) had little interaction with any women other than those native to the land. Over the colonial era an interdependent society emerged, in which the whites and Native Americans were bound together by economics and kinship. Essentially, the fur traders who married native women adopted Indian ways of life. "Wherever Europeans and native peoples came into contact, Indian women were fundamental links in the chain of mutual exchanges, mutual suspicions, and mutual understandings that bond their two peoples together," writes Jane Kamensky. "Like Pocahontas, native women were not just translators of foreign words. They were also translators of the differences between the

Pocahontas pleads with her father to spare John Smith's life.

so-called 'old' and 'new' worlds—translators of culture."[9]

Mediators and Peace Brokers

The women—and children—of these interracial marriages often formed a bridge between colonial and Native American cultures, serving as mediators, interpreters, and advisers to both sides. For example, Madame Montour (whose first name is unknown), the daughter of a French father and an Iroquois mother, served as an interpreter in negotiations between the Iroquois and colonies of New York and Pennsylvania in the early 1700s.

In the 1730s, Mary Musgrove (née Cousaponokesa), a Creek who married a prominent South Carolina colonist, served as official interpreter and adviser to James Ogelthorpe, who was establishing the new colony of Georgia. When her husband, John Musgrove, died, he left her a five-hundred-acre plantation and a thriving deerskin business. Mary soon became one of the wealthiest and most influential women on the Georgia frontier. For several decades, Mary Musgrove continued to use her influence

James Ogelthorpe established the colony of Georgia. Ogelthorpe's interpreter and trusted adviser was Mary Musgrove, a Creek woman.

in attempts to forge an alliance between the colonies and neighboring Native American groups.

Nanye'hi also changed the course of history. She had become a Beloved Woman of the Cherokee nation after bravely taking up her dead husband's musket and fighting alongside the other warriors during a raid on a Creek village. In 1757 Nanye'hi married white trader Bryant Ward and assumed the name Nancy Ward. In the decades to come, as violence between white colonists and Native American villages escalated, Nancy Ward fought for peace. In one dramatic incident, she called upon her status as a Beloved Woman to save the life of a white woman who was about to be burned at the stake. She often slipped away from her village to warn the white settlers of a raid and provided food for hungry white soldiers.

Peace was difficult to broker. Over the next several decades, the Cherokee nation waged a bloody campaign to defend its homeland from white encroachment. In 1785 Nancy Ward joined thirty-seven Cherokee men to meet with the whites to settle their disputes. At the treaty signing, the Cherokee representatives asked Ward to speak. "I hope that you have now taken us by the hand in real friendship," she told the white commissioners. "I look on you and the red people as my children. . . . The talk I have given is for the young warriors I have raised in my town, as well as myself. They rejoice that we have peace, and we hope the chain of friendship will never be broken."[10]

Sachems and Queens

It may have been unusual for a Native American woman to broker a peace with the colonists, but it was not unheard of. Cockacoeske, a descendant of Powhatan whom the English called Queen Anne, ruled the Powhatan Confederacy from the 1650s to the 1680s. During her rule, she signed a peace agreement with the neighboring English colonies that lasted until the American Revolution.

A woman known to historians as the Squaw Sachem of Massachusetts was another seventeenth-century leader who had to deal with the new white settlers living on lands once considered her tribe's. The wife of Nanapashemet, a powerful leader who came to rule over most of the Native American groups in present-day Massachusetts, Maine, and New Hampshire, Squaw Sachem assumed control over three New England tribes—the Naumkeag, the Saugus, and the Winnisimmit—upon Nanapashemet's death. She united these tribes under the old name of Massachusetts and led them in resistance to the encroachment of white settlers for more than twenty years.

Over time, these women were joined by many others who saw the threat of white encroachment on Indian agricultural lands and hunting grounds. In all the colonies, the frontier was marked by ongoing conflict between Native Americans and new settlers—conflicts characterized by raids on villages and surprise ambushes of hunting parties or other travelers, attacks and counterattacks on the innocent and guilty alike.

The conflict was not confined to warfare between whites and Indians, however. Native American tribes continued to fight one another for the prime hunting grounds. As demand for North American furs soared in England, the competition for furs aggravated tensions among various groups, particularly those in the Great Lakes region. The complex trading alliances also enmeshed the Native Americans in the ongoing rivalry between the French and English—a rivalry played out on American soil in a series of wars (King William's War, 1689–1697; Queen Anne's War, 1702–1713; King George's War, 1744–1748; and the French and Indian War, 1754–1763).

Although the warriors were predominantly male, women were by no means removed from the effects of this ongoing hostility. As conflict between the Indian and the white man grew, women and children were among the victims. Homes were burned; entire towns sacked. Those who lived there—old and young, male and female—were killed or taken captive. Women on both sides learned how to protect themselves and their children, taking up any weapon at their disposal.

White Captives

Almost a third of those taken captive by Native American groups during the colonial era remained with their captors. In *First Generations: Women in Colonial America,* historian Carol Berkin summarizes historians' differing views on why so many whites chose to stay:

> Age rather than gender was the key factor in determining a captive's fate. Those over twenty were more likely to be returned than younger colonists. But men were more likely than women to escape or to die. Women were considerably more likely than men to remain with their captors, especially if they were turned over to the French in Canada. As one historian put it, men resisted; women adapted.
>
> Why did women adapt and survive in greater numbers than their husbands, sons,

or fathers? One-fifth of the women seized … were pregnant or were carrying a nursing baby. Two lives, therefore, were at stake, and this may well have made the captive women less willing to behave rashly. …

> Other historians read the adaptation of these women as acts of rebellion against their prescribed place in Puritan society. Those women who, on ransom and release from their Indian captors, pleaded to remain or stole away from the campfires of their "rescuers" to return to their Indian families and friends may support such an interpretation. Despite the Puritan's sure sense of the superiority of his culture over Indian society, some women found the gendered division of labor and of rights and duties [among the Native Americans] more desirable than those of [white colonial communities].

Women also occasionally participated in the raids. Wetamo, who became sachem of Pocasset when her father died in 1665, opposed the encroachment of the white colonists on native lands. Although she maintained peace for a decade, when her brother-in-law Metacomet called for war in 1675, she allied herself with him, even though that meant leaving her second husband, who had declared his loyalty to England. Under her lead, hundreds of war-

riors joined with other Native American tribes of New England in raids on white villages. The series of attacks and counterattacks that became known as King Philip's War resulted in the deaths of an estimated two thousand Native Americans and six hundred whites.

Captives

Colonists who were not killed in raids on their villages were taken captive. Between

1675 and 1763, more than sixteen hundred whites became Native American captives in New England alone. At least a third of these prisoners were women; many more were children.

Captivity narratives abound with dramatic accounts of capture by Native American tribes and horrors endured by the captives. Women were dragged from their homes and forced to march a hundred miles or more. Hannah Swarton, taken captive by a tribe of Abenaki, wrote of traveling "over steep and hideous Mountains one while [day] and another while over Swamps and Thickets of Fallen trees, lying one, two, three foot from the ground, which I have stepped on, from one to another, nigh a thousand in a day; carrying a great Burden on my Back."[11] Those who could not keep up the pace were often killed by their captors. Babies, considered a burden that would slow down the retreating captors, might be hanged from a tree or otherwise murdered. In writing about events in New England in 1699, famed minister Cotton Mather wrote that one woman's three-week-old son was dashed against a tree and thrown into the river, after which the mother was told that "she was now eased of her burden and must walk faster than she did before!"[12]

The Native Americans held some captives in the hope of collecting a ransom from their families. During the series of skirmishes known as King Philip's War, Mary Rowlandson, a Massachusetts settler, watched in horror as Indians burned her home in Lancaster, Massachusetts, killed twelve people hiding within, and captured her and twenty-three others (including three of her children). After being forced to march over 150 miles through the winter snow, Rowlandson was held as a slave for over eleven weeks before being ransomed to her husband for twenty pounds. Her story is not unique, but she became an instant celebrity after she published an account of the events called *The Narrative of the Captivity and Restoration of Mrs. Mary Rowlandson.*

Mary Rowlandson shields her child from attacking Indians. Rowlandson was captured and held captive for eleven weeks.

Some captive women were also used in diplomatic negotiations. After spending a year as a captive of the Abenaki during King Philip's War, Elizabeth Hammon wrote and delivered a letter from her captors describing terms by which they would release their prisoners. Captive Goody Stockford also returned to her community with a message from her captors, and then went back to the Indians with goods to be used to buy back other prisoners.

Remaining with the Natives

A few captives in Native American communities, especially children, were adopted to replace loved ones who had been killed or captured. Once adopted, Native Americans treated the newcomers like members of the family. Mary Jemison explains that she was adopted as a substitute for a lost child, was renamed, and "was ever considered and treated by [her new family] as a real sister, the same as though I had been born of their mother."[13]

Some white colonists, usually those who had been captured as children, chose to remain among their captors even when offered their freedom. In New England, an estimated 30 percent of those taken captive by Native Americans remained among them for good. Figures show that more girls than boys remained with the Indians. The youngest daughter of John Williams, who with her father was taken prisoner in the

The Work of Native American Women

Kidnapped and adopted by the Seneca in 1758, young Mary Jemison was among the women who chose not to return home. In the following account, reprinted in Sara M. Evans's *Born for Liberty,* Jemison describes the work of the Native American women:

We pursued our farming business according to the general custom of Indian women, which is as follows: In order to expedite their business, and at the same time enjoy each other's company, they all work together in one field, or at whatever job they may have on hand. In the spring, they choose an old active squaw to be their driver and overseer, when at labor, for the ensuing year. She accepts the honor, and they consider themselves bound to obey her.

When the time for planting arrives, and the soil is prepared, the squaws are assembled in the morning, and conduced into a field where each plants one row. They then go into the next field and plant once across, and so on till they have gone through the tribe.

Mary Neff, Samuel Lennardson, and Hannah Duston (left to right) gain their freedom. They killed and scalped several of their Indian captors before escaping.

early 1700s, was one example. Kidnapped as a young child, she soon learned the habits and customs of her captors and, offered freedom repeatedly, steadfastly refused to return to her white family. She eventually married a Native American and insisted until the end that she preferred life as an Indian.

Fighting Back

Of course, those who chose to stay with their captors were a minority. Many women returned home after being ransomed by husbands or other relatives. A few gained their freedom by stealing away. Fewer still fought back and won.

One of the most famous accounts of a woman gaining her freedom through force was that of Hannah Duston. In 1697 Indians attacked the village of Haverhill, Massachusetts, and took about forty people captive, including Duston, her five-day-old infant, and Duston's midwife, Mary Neff. Duston and her colleagues were forced to march over one hundred miles into the wilderness. Hannah Duston's infant died in the Indian camp, but Duston retaliated. With the help of Neff and a boy named Samuel Lennardson, she killed her captors. Pausing only to take their scalps—for which the colonial government offered a monetary reward—Duston, Neff, and Lennardson fled for home.

Other women battled Indians in an attempt to defend their children. Historian

William Fowler tells the story of an eighteenth-century Vermont woman who fought back after a band of Indians attacked her house and carried off her children:

> With pallid, face, flashing eyes, and lips compressed, maternal love dominating every fear, she strode into the Indian camp, regardless of the tomahawks menacingly flourished round her head, boldly demanded the release of her little ones, and persevered in her alternate upbraidings and supplications, till her request was granted. [14]

The Decline of a People

All along the colonial frontier, these dramas were played out as Native Americans continued to raid villages and wage war to defend their land from encroachment. But they could do little against the onslaught of Europeans who crossed the Atlantic Ocean in search of a better life. Upon the heels of the first fledgling settlements in the early 1600s, wave after wave of Europeans joined their brothers and sisters in the New World.

Life for the Native Americans was forever changed by contact with European settlers. Native American villages were immediately devastated by smallpox, measles, and a host of other diseases against which they had acquired no immunity. As early as 1620, the Native American population in Massachusetts had been reduced by almost two-thirds, and entire villages had been wiped out.

The new colonists believed that this devastation was a sign from God that these lands were theirs for the taking. Mary Smith, a Pennsylvania Quaker, wrote in the early eighteenth century, "God's providence made room for us in a wonderful manner, in taking away the Indians. There came a distemper [sickness] among them so mortal that they could not bury all the dead. Others went away, leaving their town." [15]

Contact with Europeans and European goods also eroded traditional ways of life. Native Americans quickly seized on the opportunity to trade furs, food, shells, and even land for metal kettles, tools, and needles. The indigenous peoples quickly became dependent on European tools and lost their age-old tradition of crafting their own axes, knives, and arrowheads from stone. As one historian explains:

> As the people grew accustomed to metal tools, they lost the arts of chipping flint into arrowheads and shaping pieces of bone into knives and scrapers. As a result, foreign-made articles that began as luxuries were soon necessities. Without metal farm tools, Indian villagers could not raise enough food to sustain themselves. They were growing dependent on the white traders for their very survival. [16]

On the "Noble Savage"

❧

Most Europeans believed that the Native Americans were uncivilized savages. However, not all colonists agreed with this supposition. Here, Anne Grant, who wrote of her experiences as a child in New York, gives a different view of the Native Americans. The following is reprinted from Selma R. Williams's *Demeter's Daughters:*

> On the Mohawk River, about forty miles from Albany . . . were the once renowned Five Nations, whom anyone who remembers them while they were a people, will hesitate to call savages. Were they savages who had fixed habitation; who cultivated rich fields; who built castles (for so they called their not incommodious wooden houses, surrounded with palisades); who planted maize and beans, and showed considerable ingenuity in constructing and adorning their canoes, arms, and clothing? They who had wise though unwritten laws, and conducted their wars, treaties, and alliances with deep and sound policy . . . whose language was sonorous, musical, and expressive, who possessed generous and elevated sentiments, heroic fortitude, and unstained probity [decency].

The traditional Native American division of labor and the lives and work of both men and women also underwent a drastic transformation. Historian Sara M. Evans sums up the changes: "As cultural, economic, and military contacts [with whites] grew, the differences between women and men in each group began to change. In some cases women appropriated new sources of wealth and power; in others they lost both skills and autonomy."[17]

Of course, life would change drastically for those who came to the American continent from Europe as well. Even as the colonists looked at the Native Americans' division of labor with disgust and disdain, they soon found that their preconceived notions about what was appropriate women's work would not hold in the so-called New World. If the colonies were to survive, women would have to take on new responsibilities—responsibilities that were seen as unsuitable for women in the established Old World communities from which they came.

Chapter 2:
Colonial Women in the Home and Family

❦

Like the Native American women who preceded them, most of the European women who settled along the coast of North America engaged in a wide range of tasks. By far, most colonial women's tasks were domestic. Preparing meals, making clothing, cleaning the house, churning butter, making soap and candles, caring for and training children—these were the responsibilities of the colonial housewife.

From the beginning, women toiled in ways they would have considered unthinkable in Europe. In Europe it was considered improper for women to work out-of-doors, even among the poorest families, but women throughout colonial America joined men in the fields. In his account of the settlement of Plymouth, Massachusetts, colonial founder William Bradford writes, "The women went willingly to the field to get corn, taking their little ones with them."[18]

This story was repeated throughout the colonies. Historian Selma R. Williams writes, "The Dutch women of New Netherland in the 1620s and 1630s worked alongside their husbands building log huts thatched with straw. They also cultivated grain, harvested crops, and quickly learned to use a rifle against attacking animals or Indians."[19] Farther south, comments historian Jane Kamensky, "The Chesapeake planter's wife could not afford to center her labors around her house and its surrounding yards. Particularly if she were indentured under or married to the poorer sort of planter, the daily chores of the English woman in Virginia or Maryland were likely to include work in the fields."[20]

In Virginia, Maryland, and other colonies, men vastly outnumbered women for decades after settlement. The resulting imbalance, writes Kamensky, "meant that English notions of the proper sexual division of labor simply *could* not apply. In a colony where land was abundant and labor was scarce, a certain degree of flexibility regarding one's day-to-day tasks was an absolute necessity. Vast fields were all but begging for hands to plant them. It was almost a foregone conclusion that some of those hands would be women's."[21]

Wives Wanted!

In the first Puritan colonies in Massachusetts, the immigrants came in family groups. Among those aboard the *Mayflower* were twenty-eight females (eighteen wives, eight girls, and two maidservants). Three of the women were pregnant, one of whom —Elizabeth Hopkins—gave birth on the voyage. As other Puritans left England, they too traveled in family groups.

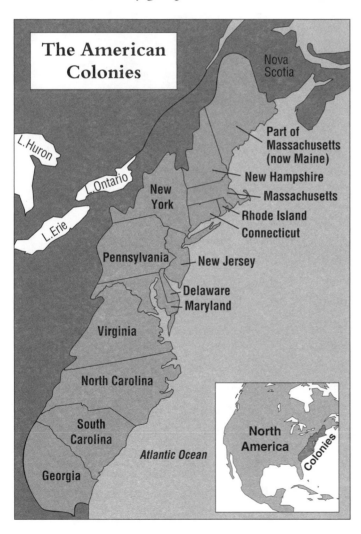

The American Colonies

Nova Scotia

L. Huron

L. Ontario

L. Erie

New York

Part of Massachusetts (now Maine)

New Hampshire

Massachusetts

Rhode Island

Connecticut

Pennsylvania

New Jersey

Delaware

Maryland

Virginia

North Carolina

South Carolina

Atlantic Ocean

Georgia

North America

Colonies

Although Plymouth and the neighboring Puritan colonies included women from the beginning, Jamestown and other early settlements of Virginia were settled by adventurers seeking their fortune, almost all of whom were men. Edwin Sandys, a leader of Jamestown, concluded that the "want of wives [was among] the greatest of hindrances" to the success of the new plantation. He added his hope that a shipment of "an extraordinarily choice lot of . . . maides" would help "make the men more settled and lesse moveable."[22]

In November 1619 the communities in Virginia enlisted the help of agents in Europe to entice women to the colony. The male colonists offered to pay for passage across the Atlantic, where women could find not only husbands, but riches as well. The promise struck a chord in England, where the economy was flagging. Within three years, nearly 150 Englishwomen, most of whom were young, poor, and alone, ventured across the Atlantic in response to Virginia's solicitations. By the end of 1622, every one of them had married.

For the next several decades, Virginia and her neighbors continued to persuade women to leave England for the colonies.

Unmarried female settlers arrive in Jamestown. European women were enticed to the colonies with promises of husbands and land grants.

To encourage the settlement of Maryland, Cecil Calvert, Lord Baltimore, promised each adult—woman and man alike—one hundred acres, and each child an additional fifty acres. In 1666 an agent working for the colonies appealed to women to help settle "South Virginia" (present-day North Carolina), writing, "If any maid or single woman have a desire to go over, they will think themselves in the Golden Age, when men paid a dowry for their wives; for if they be but civil and under fifty years of age, some honest man or other will purchase them for their wives."[23]

New World Hardships

Life was in some ways much harder than the adventurous women who traveled the New World had anticipated. In fact, many women did not survive their first few years in the colonies. Only four of the eighteen wives who left Europe on the *Mayflower* survived the first winter in Plymouth, and an estimated three-quarters of the women who traveled to Virginia between 1619 and 1622 died within five years of starvation and disease. Historians Eleanor Flexner and Ellen Fitzpatrick sum up the travails of the colonial woman:

While the men hunted, chopped, built, plowed, fought the Indians, and sat in council together, the women cared for one another in childbirth and sickness with no skill to call on save their own, wrestled with strange foods in a [savage] climate . . . ; they toiled from sunup to sundown, converting the raw skins and meat brought home by the men into the necessary food and clothing and tended the ground the men had cleared.[24]

Those who lived described the hardships they encountered and overcame. Judith Giton, who settled in South Carolina in 1685, wrote in a letter home to France,

"Everything went wrong. Our elder brother died of the fever. We bore every kind of affliction, illness, plague, hunger, poverty, and hard work. I have had no bread to eat for six months and have tilled the soil like a slave."[25] Almost a century later, Mary Cooper, who lived on a family farm in Oyster Bay, New York, wrote in her diary in 1769, "This day is forty years since I left my father's house and come here, and I have seene little else but hard labor and much sorrow. . . . I am dirty and tired almost to death."[26]

Marriage and Childbirth

Virtually every woman of seventeenth- and eighteenth-century America got married. Most women married young, except

A couple dances at their wedding. Almost all women in colonial America married young and remarried if widowed.

for those who made the passage from Europe as indentured servants, who were forbidden to marry until they had completed their indenture, usually a period of four to seven years. Married women were expected to establish their own households upon marriage, taking on the many duties that this involved. They were also expected and legally bound in many ways to to obey their husbands and defer to his decision.

The average woman in colonial America had a baby about fifteen months after marriage and gave birth every two years thereafter. Giving birth was as dangerous as it was common. Approximately one in five women died during childbirth. Those who survived childbirth typically bore eight or nine children; as many as twelve or thirteen was not uncommon. But rarely did all of a family's children reach adulthood. An estimated one-quarter of all children born in the Chesapeake region during the 1600s died in infancy, and only about three-quarters of the children born in seventeenth-century New England, and less than half in Virginia and Maryland, lived to the age of twenty.

A birth was attended not only by a midwife, but also by female friends and relatives. In fact, it was not unheard of for an entire community of married women to attend a delivery. Women joined together at the home of the mother-to-be when labor pains began and stayed for hours and sometimes days. "Childbirth was as central an experience for the women's community at large as for its individual members," writes historian Mary Beth Norton. "Although women often casually encountered each other during the course of their daily lives . . . only birthing rooms provided women with environments that consistently excluded men."[27]

Feeding the Family

Children were a welcome addition in most families. On the typical colonial farm, girls and boys alike helped to plant corn and other crops in the fields, reaped the harvest during the fall or at harvest time, and tended the animals. Girls helped with the housework as well, learning largely from their mothers the skills necessary to run the household and care for the family.

Throughout the colonies, fulfilling the responsibilities of a housewife usually meant spending most of the day tending to the home and fixing food for the family. In most New England homes, a huge fireplace—as large as eight feet across and five feet high—dominated one wall of a central living room–kitchen. Here, the typical colonial woman began the day at dawn stoking the fire, which was needed not only for cooking but for heat and light as well. Maintaining the fire was a round-the-clock task; wood burned quickly and untended embers could easily die out if no one was keeping watch. Historian Carl Holliday writes: "The very building of a fire to cook the food was a

A Woman's Work Is Never Done

It was difficult for colonial men to succeed without a wife. Men who found themselves widowed usually hired a woman to do the work of a housewife, at least until a new wife could be found. The following 1780 advertisement gives insight into what life would be like for domestic laborers. This excerpt is from Carl Holliday's *Woman's Life in Colonial Days*:

Wanted at a [home] about half a day's journey from Philadelphia, on which are good improvements and domestics, A single Woman of unsullied Reputation, an affable cheerful, active and amiable Disposition; cleanly, industrious, perfectly qualified to direct and manage the female Concerns of country business, as raising small stock, dairying, marketing, combing, carding, spinning, knitting, sewing, pickling, preserving, etc., and occasionally to instruct two Young Ladies in those Branches of Oeconomy [home economics], who, with their father, compose the Family. Such a person will be treated with respect and esteem, and meet with every encouragement due to such a character.

laborious task with flint and steel, one generally avoided by never allowing the embers on the family hearth to die."[28] It usually fell to the woman of the house, or a child or servant, to cover the remaining embers with ashes to keep the fire alive for rekindling.

Cooking was women's work exclusively, and colonial housewives spent much of the day preparing the day's meals. This was heavy labor. Most families used a few basic utensils: an iron skillet and a spit or two for roasting meat, as well as an iron pot for making soup, pottage, or stew. The metal pots were large and heavy, weighing as much as forty pounds. Carl Holliday calls them "implements for pre-historic giants rather than for frail women."[29]

The typical colonial meal consisted of stews of meat or fish and a combination of whatever vegetables were in season in the garden, along with homemade bread. In most homes, all baking was done just once a week, often on Saturday. In cooking, as in most elements of colonial America, women improvised, taking what they had learned in their homelands and adapting it to their new conditions. They learned also from the natives they encountered, introducing new foods such as corn to their diet. Historian Selma R. Williams writes that "the famous hoecake," a common bread in New England, "was an improvisation of the original Indian method. Early settlers used a mortar and pestle on the grain, and

A colonial family tends to their chores. Women typically spent most of the day preparing food.

then baked the dough on the broad blade of a shovel or hoe."[30]

Preparing the food was only the beginning of a colonial woman's responsibilities. Daily chores typically included tending the garden, gathering eggs from the hens, and feeding the family's chickens and other animals that were housed in small buildings in the backyard. Most families owned a cow or two, and milking the cows also was considered women's work in the New World. When the family needed meat, often a woman slaughtered the chicken, pig, or other livestock before preparing it to be cooked on the open fire. Women salted and preserved the meat that was not to be consumed immediately to be stored for the coming months. In the fall, women prepared for winter by drying fruits, preserving vegetables and fruits, and processing milk into butter and cheese, a task that took most of the day. A woman's tasks also included brewing cider or beer, the stable beverages that were consumed at almost every meal.

Colonial women became adept at diagnosing illnesses and prescribing remedies, serving as a doctor and nurse for husband and family. Those who were fortunate enough to have servants or slaves also took on responsibility for providing them with basic medical services as well. Most women made their own medicines, gathering or growing the required herbs, drying them, mixing and pureeing various ingredients into ointments or distilling them into syrups. The colonial women learned many of the remedies and techniques for making medicines from the Native Americans.

Spinning, Sewing, and So On

Most women also made the family's clothing. There were several time-consuming steps involved in this process: spinning the flax and wool into thread, weaving it into cloth, dyeing it, and piecing and sewing the desired garment. In time an increasing number of women began to purchase thread rather than spinning it themselves. This was especially true in the southern colonies, where the constancy of trade allowed ready access to manufactured and European goods. Stephanie Grauman Wolf describes how the nature of spinning

Health Tips in Colonial America

More often than not, women of colonial America served as doctor, nurse, and pharmacist to their husbands and children and sometimes to neighbors as well. The following concoctions are among several remedies reprinted in Kemp Battle's *Hearts on Fire*.

For Comforting the Head & Braine: Take Rosemary & Sage . . . , with flowers of Rosemary if to be had, & Borage with ye flowers. Infuse in Muscadine or in good Canary 3 dayes, drinke it often. The fat of a Hedg-hog roasted drop it into the Eare, is an excellent remedy against deafnes. Also a Clove of Garlick, make holes in it, dip it in Honey, & put it into the Eare at night going to bed, first on one side, then on the other for 8 or 9 dayes together, keeping in ye Eares black wooll.

For Hoarseness: Take 3 or 4 figs, cleave them in two, put in a pretty quantity of Ginger in powder, roast them & Eate them often.

To Kill Worms in Children: Take sage, boil it with milk to a good tea, turn it to whey with alum or vinegar, and give the whey to the child, if the worms are not knotted in the stomach, and it will be a sure cure. If the worms are knotted in the stomach, it will kill the child.

changed over time: "Throughout the eighteenth century, spinning became less a task for all women and more one for certain groups of women: farm women whose own homesteads produced the raw material; and poor women and children of both sexes who lived in urban communities."[31]

Even where spinning was no longer among a housewife's responsibilities, women continued to be responsible for fashioning linens and clothing from cloth. Writes Wolf,

A Recipe for Butter

Much of the work that fell to women was time-consuming, heavy labor. Here are early instructions for making butter, reprinted from *Colonial American Home Life* by John F. Warner.

As soon as you have Milked, Strain your Milk into a Pot and stir it often for Half an Hour, then put it away in your Pots or Trays. When it's Creamed, skim it exceedingly Clean from the Milk, and put your Cream into an Earthen Pot, and if you do not Churn immediately for Butter, shift your cream once in twelve hours into another clean Pot. When you have Churned, Wash your Butter in three or four Waters, then Salt it as you will have it, and Beat it well. Let it stand in a Wedge . . . till the next Morning, beat it again and make your Layers the thickness of three Fingers, and then throw a little Salt on it. And so do until your Pot is full.

Three women work together to make butter.

"Women were expected to be skillful with shears for cutting cloth, and with the needle for sewing it together. It was they who made the sheets, napkins, bed-curtains, and cushions used in the house; they who made the basic family clothes."[32]

Washing the family's clothes was a laborious chore that required toting and heating large quantities of water, as well as scrubbing the clothing with harsh lye soaps. Despite the backbreaking nature of these tasks, the laundry was exclusively woman's domain. A foreign observer at an early Revolutionary War battle commented that the American soldiers' unwillingness or inability to care for their own garments resulted in their "ragged and unkempt" appearance; the men "let their linen, etc., rot upon their backs than to be at the trouble of cleaning 'em themselves."[33]

During epidemic illness, laundering was made more difficult by community-wide restrictions on where the wash could be done or how used washwater could be disposed of. During an outbreak of malaria in Jamestown in 1616, for example, the town issued the following edict: "No laundress dare to wash any unclean linen . . . or throw out the water or suds of foul clothes in the open street, within the palisades [around the town center], or within forty feet of the same."[34] Town orders also required women to drag their dirty pans and kettles to the riverbank rather than drawing water from a nearby well or pump.

Among the many other activities of the typical colonial woman was making soap and candles. The soap of the day was a mixture of animal fat and lye, which women boiled together in a huge kettle for many hours. This usually required women to first make the lye from the ashes of various hardwoods—a tedious and somewhat dangerous task, given the caustic chemical properties of lye. Making candles also fell to women, a task that Carl Holliday calls "a harsh but inevitable duty in the autumn. The lugging about of immense kettles, the smell of tallow, deer suet, bear's grease, and stale pot-liquor, and the constant demands of the great fireplace must have made the candle season a period of terror and loathing to many a burdened wife and mother."[35]

Community Life

Although a woman's work focused on home and family, it also brought her beyond her own home into the community. "Most family economies required that, in addition to production for home consumption, women produce for the market as well,"[36] explains Stephanie Grauman Wolf. Those who lived near a town or village set out once or twice a week to trade surplus cheese, eggs, butter, or garden vegetables with their neighbors to acquire items that they were unable to grow themselves.

These networks of trade and shared responsibility resulted in strengthened relationships among colonial women, and work sometimes blended with social activity: "[A woman's] arduous tasks frequently required neighborly co-operation, and social functions thus became mingled with industrial activities," explains Carl Holliday. "Quilting bees, spinning bees, knitting bees, sewing bees, paring bees, and a dozen other types of 'bees' served to lighten the drudgery of such work and developed a spirit of neighborliness."[37]

In the South, where people settled on large tracts of land, such neighborly cooperation was less common than in more densely populated regions. As described by a contemporary, southerners often "plant[ed] themselves at a distance, for the sake of having an uncultivated country around them for their cattle to range in."[38] Living on large tracts of land, a southern woman often had little or no human contact outside her husband and children. Selma R. Williams explains, "To visit as close as three miles away, a woman would have to get a horse from pasture, form some kind of halter, ride bareback, and somehow cross or swim a river bounding the property. There were few roads during the first few generations, and bad weather often made even well-worn paths impassable."[39]

The southern belle was perhaps in less need of neighbors than her contemporaries in New England. The southern colonies' emphasis on cash crops and constant trade with England and the West Indies made cloth, candles, soaps, and other household items readily available, making cooperative industry unnecessary for wealthier southerners.

But the isolation also contributed to a woman's burdens. Distance made it difficult for southerners to rely on a neighbor's expertise in caring for the sick or during childbirth. Distance between plantations and towns meant that visitors often stayed for weeks or even months at a time. Whereas northerners typically conducted business and affairs of state in meetinghouses, taverns, or

"The Pleasures of Country Life"

Although she was not poor, Ruth Belknap, a literate goodwife married to a local parson in Dover, New Hampshire, resented the growing wealth of those living in the cities and towns of colonial America. In "The Pleasures of a Country Life," a 1782 poem reprinted in Jane Kamensky's *The Colonial Mosaic,* Belknap bitterly scorned the leisurely life of townsfolk:

Ye starch'd up folks that live in town,
That lounge upon your beds till noon,
That never tire yourselves with work,
Unless with handling knife & fork,
Come, see the sweets of country life,
display'd in Parson B[elknap's] wife.

other public spaces, the distance between towns in the South led to a different culture in which men addressed such matters in one another's homes. This added to the responsibilities of the southern gentlewoman. Stephanie Grauman Wolf concludes, "We can be sure that the fifty or more people who stayed with William Byrd each month, either on his plantation or at his home in Williamsburg, were not cared for by him in anything but the figurative sense; their bed linens, their wash, their food, and any incidental sewing was done or prepared by the women of the house."[40]

To be sure, some women benefited from the assistance of servants and slaves, but a southern housewife's responsibilities were no less daunting. Only the wealthiest had house servants, and even these women had to oversee the myriad household tasks to be completed—cooking, cleaning, laundering, caring for the children, obtaining food, candles, soap, and the like.

On the southern plantation, wives and daughters were also responsible for taking care of the slaves. They fed and clothed them; they looked after the sick or infirm; they helped to deliver the babies. Even women of the most elite class directed attention to the care of their "property." A biographer of Martha Washington writes that "the welfare of the slaves, of whom one hundred and fifty had been part of her dower, their clothing, much of which was

Like other plantation mistresses, Martha Washington saw to the welfare of her plantation's slaves.

woven and made upon the estate, their comfort, especially when ill; and their instruction in sewing, knitting, and other housewifely arts, engaged much of Mrs. Washington's time and thought."[41]

Growing in Wealth

Over time, the colonial communities gained a foothold in the wilderness. Towns grew, houses grew, and wealth grew. The colonists began to acquire goods that demonstrated their improved position and refinement:

Linens, forks, silver, even chairs signified a family's rising status. By the mid–eighteenth century, the average American's life closely resembled that of his or her contemporary in England. Freed from daily chores in the fields, the colonial housewife spent most of her time engaged in traditionally feminine duties, as defined by Europeans: cooking, sewing, dairying, gardening, tending poultry and hogs, and caring for children. Wealthy women participated in the dances, teas, and other social events that were becoming increasingly common as towns and villages grew in size and sophistication.

But even among the wealthy, a woman's work was seemingly endless. Mary Holyoke, a doctor's wife living in the prosperous seaport town of Salem, Massachusetts, might be considered among the lucky elite. Yet in her diary she writes of long days spent washing and ironing, sewing and embroi-

dering, tending the garden and milking the cows, making soap and candles, curing bacon and making cheese. In one entry, she talks of her experiences butchering a 164-pound pig; in another, of churning 77 pounds of butter to set aside for the winter.

Whether gentlewomen in the northern colonies or southern ladies, women who had time for dances, teas, and other social events were a small minority. On the eve of the American Revolution, most ordinary farmers continued to eke out a living, working from dawn to dusk. And most women continued to spend their days as had the generations before them, taking care of their homes and families. Over time, however, an increasing number of these households included not only people related by blood, but also counted among them people who were hired—or enslaved—to work for them.

Chapter 3:
Servants and Slaves

Despite the strong work ethic and ingenuity of the women and men who settled the New World, there was more work to do in the American colonies than there were hands to do it. Desperate for labor, the colonies went to great extremes to attract workers to the New World. Advertisements placed in European newspapers and broadsides described a land full of riches, where land was plentiful and husbands were available for the taking. The ads appealed to poor women in England and elsewhere in Europe where work, men, and land were scarce. Thus, the colonies attracted tens of thousands of indentured servants.

Under the terms of indenture, the prospective servant agreed to work for a specified period of time—usually between four and seven years—in return for passage across the Atlantic and shelter, clothing, and food during their term of indenture. When the period of indenture ended the servant would be free to do as she pleased. Often she was given a small sum of money or plot of land on which to begin a new life. Because of the shortage of women, most female indentured servants quickly found husbands.

The colonists desperate for labor soon found a new, even more inexpensive source—the African slave. In the early days of the colonies, slavery existed in the North as well as the South, but it never took hold in the northern colonies as it did in the South, where the agricultural economy was dependent on cheap labor. By 1700 slavery was abolished in all of the colonies in New England, but it would continue throughout the South for over 160 years.

Indentured Servitude

An estimated 250,000 people—including 80,000 females—migrated to America as indentured servants. In fact, indentured servants accounted for 80 to 90 percent of the seventeenth-century emigration from England to the middle colonies, and for virtually all female emigration. Most new arrivals were from England, Ireland, and Germany.

The servants who came to the North American colonies were poor, unmarried, uneducated, and illiterate. These disadvantages made them easy targets for unscrupulous agents. Their indenture was invariably written by a third-party agent, inevitably for a higher price than they would have had to pay had they been able to negotiate directly for passage across the ocean. Actually, many indentured servants who came to the colonies in the seventeenth and eighteenth centuries were tricked into boarding the ships destined for the New World, or even kidnapped outright. Richard Hofstadter writes:

> The [recruiting agents], who worked for respectable merchants, were known to lure children with sweets, to seize upon the weak or the gin-sodden and take them aboard ship, and to bedazzle the credulous or weak-minded by fabulous promises of an easy life in the New World. Often their victims were taken roughly in hand and, pending departure, held in imprisonment either on shipboard or in low-grade hostels or brothels. [42]

From the beginning, indentured servants faced great hardship. The three-month ocean voyage was treacherous. The servants lived in cramped quarters aboard ship, making the spread of dysentery, smallpox, and other diseases quick and deadly. Some ships lacked sufficient shelter, leaving passengers exposed to inclement weather and sun. Unscrupulous captains padded their profits by nearly starving their passengers. Food spoiled and had to be thrown overboard. The dead were likewise tossed into the sea.

After weeks at sea, the passengers were no doubt relieved by the first sight of land,

but their difficulties were by no means over. Selma R. Williams describes the plight of the indentured servants:

> As the ship neared port, passengers were ordered to wash faces, clean clothes as best as possible, and tidy the

Like Africans brought to the New World to serve as slaves (pictured), indentured servants from Europe also faced a perilous ocean journey.

hair. On arrival in America, the human cargo would be displayed, inspected, picked over, and sold to the highest bidder. . . . Prospective buyers came aboard, pawed bodies from head to toe, ordered prospective servants to walk and to talk in order to judge physical stamina, morality, intelligence, and submissiveness. [43]

Some passengers were devastated to learn that the conditions of their servitude were not what they had been promised. During the voyage, the servants' terms of indenture were often lost or stolen, leaving them further at the mercy of their handlers. Families suddenly found themselves separated despite promises they could stay together; travelers found that they had been assessed additional monies for "extras" along the way. Richard Hofstadter sets the stage: "On the ships and at the docks there were final scenes of despair and frenzy as servants searched for lost articles of indenture, or lamented the disappearance of baggage, unexpected overcharges, the necessity of accepting indentures longer than their debts fairly required, the separation of families." [44]

Some masters selected their own servants on the docks or shipboard, but most servants were purchased by a middleman who then sold the indenture at a profit. Large-scale buyers bought groups of servants and marched them miles from the coast, selling them to ready masters along the way.

The Servant's Home

Once "purchased," the living conditions of indentured servants varied greatly. "Good or bad luck, the disposition of the master, the length of the term of work, the size of the plantation or farm, the robustness or frailty of the worker—all these had a part in determining the fate of each individual," [45] writes Hofstadter.

Early in the colonial period, most servants found themselves in an almost desperate situation. Conditions in the early colonial home were squalid, even by the standards of England's poor. Maidservants who were lucky were given a straw pallet in the eaves in the colonial home; others were housed in lean-tos, barns, or outdoor sheds. Meals consisted mainly of what one traveler in Virginia called a "somewhat indigestible soup." [46] Their clothing was made from coarse, homespun flax and was often inadequate.

As the colonies gained wealth and population, a lucky few were bought by wealthy families in need of an extra pair of hands or caretaker for their children. But an increasing number were put to work on plantations in southern colonies, where they served as field hands growing tobacco, rice, or indigo. Those accustomed to a milder European climate found the conditions on the southern plantation unbearable. Many of those sent to plantation fields died in the first year of service—during what came to be known as their "seasoning"—from malaria, dysentery, and other diseases.

Devious masters sometimes took advantage of their servants' relative ignorance and lack of support in their new environment to exploit their indenture. Many indentures, for example, required a master to provide the servant with basic education, a provision that was routinely ignored. Often, masters sought to maximize their investment in the servant by providing as little food and clothing as possible. A young servant in the Chesapeake region lamented her plight in a letter to her father back in England:

> What we unfortunat English People suffer here is beyond the probility of you in England to conceive . . . toiling almost Day and Night, . . . and then tied up and whipp'd to that Degree that you'd not serve an Annimal, scarce any thing but Indian Corn and Salt to eat . . . almost naked no shoes nor stockings to wear . . . what rest we can get is to wrap ourselves up in a Blanket and ly upon the Ground, this is the deplorable Conditions your poor Betty endures. [47]

In addition to the harsh treatment of servants in general, female servants were often subjected to unwelcome sexual advances of male masters.

Servants who protested their unfair treatment usually went unheard, but there were exceptions. Catherine Douglas of Lancaster, Virginia, took her master to court in 1700 for trying to hold her to seven years' service instead of freeing her at the end of four. Her master showed a document that said she had promised to serve for seven years, but she said this was not the original indenture. Several witnesses came to her defense, testifying that they had seen the original contract and that it had an indenture period of four years. The court found in her favor and ordered her to be freed.

Marriage and Family

Indentured servants were forbidden to marry, but many seemed to ignore that prohibition. Some servants married in secret; others carried on sexual liaisons outside of marriage. A few servants even found freedom through marriage. In 1643, for example, two maidservants in Virginia ran away to Maryland. By the time their master found them, the two women were both married to men who refused to return them.

The many illegitimate children born to indentured servants served as undeniable proof of illicit liaisons. Although each colony had its own laws about dealing

An indentured servant comforts an infant. As the colonies grew in wealth, some families hired such servants to help with household and family responsibilities.

with breaches of indenture contracts, most colonies meted out harsh punishments to servants who bore children during their indenture. The typical punishment was to add time to the indenture. In most colonies, servants had to serve an additional year, far longer than the few weeks they might have missed during pregnancy and childbirth. And additional time was sometimes assessed to compensate for a midwife or other expenses paid by a master during the pregnancy.

Some communities sought to further deter sexual activity among indentured servants through corporal punishment. A historian of seventeenth-century Virginia describes how that colony dealt with indentured servants who had a child out of wedlock:

If a woman gave birth to a bastard, the sheriff as soon as he learned of the fact was required to arrest her, and whip her on the bare back until the blood came. Being turned over to her

Women for Sale

Female slaves were desirable for their ability not only to work but also to bear children, as shown in the following advertisement reprinted in *Century of Struggle,* by Eleanor Flexner and Ellen Fitzpatrick.

Negroes for Sale: A girl about twenty years of age (raised in Virginia) and her two female children, one four and the other two years old—remarkably strong and healthy—Never having had a day's sickness with the exception of the small-pox, in her life. The children are fine and healthy. She is very prolific in her generating qualities and affords a rare opportunity to any person who wishes to raise a family of strong and healthy servants for their own use.

A man inspects female slaves for sale. Female slaves were valued for their ability to bear children.

master, she was compelled to pay two thousand pounds of tobacco, or to remain in his employment two years after the termination of her indentures.

Servants suspected of a liaison with black slaves faced even harsher punishment: "If the bastard child . . . was the offspring of a negro father," the historian continues, "she was whipped unless the usual fine was paid, and immediately upon the expiration of her term was sold by the wardens of the nearest church for a period of five years. . . . The child was bound out until his or her thirtieth year had been reached."[48]

Sold into Slavery

If life was difficult for the maidservant, it was brutal for the average African immigrant, particularly as slavery usurped indenture as the main source of labor in the southern colonies. For example, indentured servants had some protections under the law that black slaves did not. Indentured servants could petition the court; African slaves could not. Whipping was common among both, but severe, disfiguring beating of an indentured servant was prohibited. Codes for black slavery, on the other hand, allowed masters to inflict the harshest corporal punishment on slaves. The laws regulating slave owners presumed that a master would not willfully destroy his own property, including slaves, and therefore did not consider the death of a slave who was being punished to be murder.

The first black slaves were bought in Jamestown in 1619, just twelve years after its settlement. By 1670 most ship owners and agents were turning their attention away from the importation of indentured servants in favor of the importation of black slaves, and by the turn of the century, roughly two-thirds of the bound laborers in Maryland and Virginia were from Africa. By 1760 about 284,000 black slaves lived in the southern colonies from Maryland to Georgia, and an additional 41,000 lived in the colonies to the north. In South Carolina, African Americans made up 60 percent of the population.

Virtually all of the black slaves brought from Africa were kidnapped. Unlike indentured servants, they had neither an agent representing them nor paperwork outlining their responsibilities. A few were freed after a period of service, but most would live out the remainder of their years as slaves.

If they survived, that is. Up to a fifth of the Africans packed onto the slave ships died on the trip across the Atlantic—the so-called Middle Passage. Others succumbed to disease and malnourishment soon after landing. The death toll is not surprising given the horrid conditions of the ships carrying their black cargo. The slaves were crowded onto the ships and chained together below deck. Disease and death

Phillis Wheatley

Phillis Wheatley, the slave girl educated and encouraged by her wealthy owners, John and Susannah Wheatley, became a sensation in Boston in 1770 after she wrote a poem eulogizing George Whitefield, a renowned preacher. In 1773, thirty-nine of her poems were published as *Poems on Various Subjects, Religious and Moral*—the first book published by a black American. She went to England upon the book's release, but her visit was cut short by the illness of Susannah Wheatley, who died shortly thereafter.

Upon her return, Phillis Wheatley, like so many other women, became swept up in the revolutionary fervor gripping the colonies. In 1775 she sent a letter to commander in chief George Washington, enclosing a poem she had written in his honor. Washington—a slave owner—wrote back to the African American teen to thank her. A few months later, Wheatley's poem was published in the *Pennsylvania Magazine.*

But Phillis Wheatley's fame was fleeting. By 1778 John Wheatley also had died, and Phillis was on her own. She married John Peters, a free African American, and had three children, none of whom survived infancy. Although the couple was free of the shackles of slavery, they were not free of prejudice. They struggled to eke out a living, but Peters proved unable to find steady work. Phillis Wheatley continued to write her poetry but, without a white benefactor to support her, she could not find a publisher. Within five years, Phillis found herself alone once again (it is believed her husband was sent to debtor's prison) and working as a servant in a boarding house. She died in obscurity at the age of thirty-one.

Phillis Wheatley was the first black American to publish a book.

spread quickly on the filthy ships; food and water ran short or spoiled.

At first, most of the slaves were male. But by the end of the seventeenth century, slaveholders had realized that owning women was a good investment. Male slaves might be able to work harder in the fields, but women had children, thereby providing their owners with more slaves who could be forced into labor or sold. According to one account, "packed spoon-fashion, [the women slaves] often gave birth to children in the scalding perspiration from the human cargo."[49] By the mid-1700s, most slave ships carried one woman for every two men.

A New Home

The plight of the slave varied greatly, depending on the circumstances in which she found herself. In the North, the few black female slaves who were hired to help with housework and children were sometimes treated as a member of the family. Phillis Wheatley was among those who found herself in this position. Thrown onto a slave ship in 1761, the scrawny child (estimated to be about seven years of age) was purchased by John Wheatley, a wealthy Boston cloth merchant, and his wife, Susannah. Susannah Wheatley was so impressed by Phillis's superior intelligence that she raised her as a daughter. Susannah Wheatley taught Phillis to read and encouraged her in her love of writing poetry.

But most slaves were far less fortunate. In the South, where most Africans disembarked, the vast majority of slaves toiled in the fields. From dawn to dusk, women worked alongside men planting, tending, and harvesting the crops—usually, tobacco and corn in Virginia, indigo and rice farther south. When night fell, the slaves continued to ready the crops for market, stripping the tobacco leaves, shucking the corn, washing the indigo, pounding the rice.

The wealthiest planters owned huge plantations and a hundred or more slaves; in mid–eighteenth-century Georgia, most plantation slaves never saw a white person. But there were many more small farms with fewer than twenty slaves, and poor planters who struggled to scratch out a living with just one or two slaves could be found throughout the South. Although these slaves were sometimes spared the backbreaking work of the plantation, they were far more likely to find themselves without shelter or food than their plantation counterparts.

As time went on, planters took advantage of new technologies and better tools. Female slaves benefited little from such advances. Toward the end of the eighteenth century, male slaves were assigned to new skilled and semiskilled tasks, but women continued working as before. Carol Berkin writes:

While men plowed and mastered crafts, women remained in the fields, left to hoe by hand what the plows could not reach, to weed and worm the tobacco and to carry the harvested grain to the barns on their heads or backs. When new tasks were added to women's work repertoire, they proved to be the least desirable: building fences, grubbing swamps in the winter, cleaning seed out of winnowed grain, breaking new ground too rough for the plow, cleaning stables, and spreading manure. [50]

The Big House

A few women—often the very young, old, or infirm—worked in the plantation manor. In the so-called big house, a female slave's responsibilities included everything a colonial housewife would be expected to do—preparing the meals, cleaning the house, washing the clothes, toting water and wood, making soap and candles. Although in some cases life as a household slave was easier than as a fieldworker, the hours were long. And, while slaves working in the field often had Sundays off, house servants were expected to work seven days a week. In fact, Sundays were often unusually hectic because visitors often arrived on Sundays and many southern homes had to accommodate large numbers of overnight or dinner guests.

In addition, a few slaves had special responsibilities for caring for their owners' children. Some served as wet nurses, suckling newborns not their own. Toddlers were turned over to the nursery under the care of another slave, often an elderly, trusted house slave. In many families, black slaves often played a larger role in rearing children than did their own mothers, who were busy managing the household affairs and overseeing servants and slaves.

The Slave Family

Female plantation slaves also added to their list of responsibilities caring for the rough quarters they called home. The slave quarters were usually situated a distance from the plantation manor and usually consisted of a series of one-room huts with dirt floors and little or no furniture. Each hut was shared by several people, who may or may not have been related to one another. Here the women of the plantation sought to carve out a life for themselves and their families. "Women field hands generally had a longer day than their men," concludes historian Eugene D. Genovese. "In addition to the usual work load, the women had to cook for their families, put the children to bed, and often spin, weave, and sew well into the night." [51] Under these circumstances, slave women did their best to nourish themselves and their families. Where possible, they tended small gardens to supplement the poor food they were provided by their masters.

A few slaves, like the two pictured here, worked in the plantation manor where their many duties included looking after their owner's children.

Marriage between slaves was not recognized by law but was often sanctioned by their masters, who benefited from such relationships. The children of slaves became the property of the owner (the mother's owner in the rare instances in which the father was owned by someone else). Masters were often reluctant to separate young children from their mothers, and children were not worth much on the slave market until they could undertake enough work to pay for their upkeep. As a result, children usually lived with their mothers until they were at least ten years old.

Like their white counterparts, black babies often succumbed to disease and died before reaching their first birthday. But a slave mother faced another harsh reality as well: Her children, or the father of her children, could be taken from her at any time if the master decided to sell them. Despite these obstacles, most slaves were devoted to their children, teaching them how to survive the harsh conditions in which they lived. Like their African ancestors, most slaves nursed their babies well into their second or third year, taking them with them into the fields.

Mothers also tenaciously defended their children against white abuse at their own expense. One South Carolina slave remembered her mother thus:

My mammy, she work in da field all day and piece and quilt all night. . . . I never see how my mamy stand such hard work. She stand up for her chillen though. De old overseer he hate my mammy, 'cause she fought him for beatin' her chllen. Why she get more whippin' for dat dan any-thin' else. [52]

The Slave Community

Despite the many obstacles to forging bonds with one another, slaves in most regions of the country had a strong sense of community, both within and beyond the homes in which they lived. As slaves were

The Status of Female Slaves

Particularly in the Chesapeake region, slave women were sought for their ability to bear and raise children. A fertile woman in her child-bearing years often escaped the brutal treatment of her peers. The following excerpt is from *Century of Struggle*, by Eleanor Flexner and Ellen Fitzpatrick:

The female slave faced . . . hazards peculiar to her sex. She was used for breeding purposes to increase her owner's labor force or his stock of saleable merchandise; under existing conditions of slave life and medical care, she had to give birth often to meet both requirements. She had, more-over, no defense against the sexual advances of any white man, a fact attested to by the widespread presence of mulat-toes, some 588,000 according to the Census of 1860. . . .

Although the African matriarchal pattern had been largely destroyed, slave life itself gave the Negro woman a unique status. It was not only that, in the constant flux of slave relations, her relationship to her children was clear while the father's was often not, but also that, in addition to her capacity as a worker, the owner profited from her child-bearing and rearing her young. She was therefore less apt to be sold out of hand than the male, and was the more stable element in what little there was of slave family life. As a rule the Negro woman as wife and mother was the mistress of her cabin, and, save for the interference of master or overseer, her wishes in regard to mating and family matters were para-mount. Neither economic necessity nor tradition had instilled in her the spirit of subordination to masculine authority.

sold, dense networks of kinship evolved in the southern states. In places where slave owners' regulations permitted it, fathers traveled several miles every Sunday to spend their only free time with their families.

This interdependence and the inter-plantation community gave rise to an independent, internal slave economy. Like their white counterparts, industrious slave women could improve the station of their families by trading with one another. In the Chesapeake region, for example, women sold surplus crops from the plots that surrounded the slave quarters, as well as poultry and eggs, baked goods, garden products, or handmade baskets. Items for trade might also include animals that the slaves had hunted or trapped and goods that had been "liberated" (stolen) from the big house. Trading partners included not only slaves on one's own plantation, but slaves on other plantations, traders who traveled through the region, and even white masters or mistresses. Some slave women paid their masters a fee for the privilege of selling to others the pies, cakes, and handcrafts they made.

The slave economy was even stronger on the plantations farther south. Because rice cultivation did not require constant supervision, slaves often worked out of sight of an overseer or owner. Often the slaves were given the responsibility for cultivating the rice in a plot of land and were allowed to set their own schedule. The slaves took advantage of this freedom to grow crops for sale outside the plantation. The practice persisted despite laws that forbade slaves to market crops to anyone except their master. In addition to corn, potatoes, tobacco, peanuts, melons, and pumpkins, slaves on the rice plantations of South Carolina and Georgia grew peppers and other food crops brought with them from Africa. "When local slave crops reached Charleston," Carol Berkin writes, "slave women took charge of their marketing. These female traders were known for their shrewdness in bargaining with customers of both races, to whom they hawked poultry, eggs, and fruit at sometimes shocking prices."[53]

Runaways and Rebellion

The biggest problems for masters of indentured servants and slaves alike was the constant threats of runaways and rebellion. In southern communities where black slaves outnumbered whites, masters worried that servants and slaves would rise up against the master class. Several colonies thus passed laws that required indentured servants to carry identification and a certificate of passage (stating when and where the person was allowed to travel) whenever they left the plantation.

Masters offered substantial rewards for information leading to the capture of a runaway indentured servant and threatened anyone harboring a fugitive with court action. Upon capture, indentured servants were kept in jail until their masters could retrieve them. Time, sometimes as much as several years, was added to their indenture period as punishment; a Maryland law of 1661 added ten days to the indenture for every one missed. A maidservant in Anne Arundel County, Maryland, who ran off frequently for short periods of time was assessed 1,330 days of extra service after her master took her to court for an accumulated absence of 133 days. In some places, whipping was common. To dissuade servants from repeating the offense and make identification of runaways easier, masters sometimes used a hot iron to brand servants (an "R" was often used to identify a runaway).

Slaves too ran away, although the chance of reaching freedom was even less likely and the punishment was even harsher. Notices of runaways were published in newspapers and posted on the walls of taverns and public buildings. Dogs and bounty hunters were enlisted to track them down.

Yet some people persevered in their attempts to escape life as a slave. Runaways sometimes shot themselves or cut their throats rather than returning to their captors. Slave owners often whipped or even burned their slaves to keep them from being tempted to flee again. Slaves who ran away in Virginia or North Carolina might be sold "down river" to the Deep South, where both the working conditions and the route to freedom were even harsher.

For slaves who had children, however, the ties of motherhood were often stronger than the threats of the slave owners. Such slaves might rebel in more subtle ways, such as feigning sickness. Landon Carter, a Virginia planter, for example, wrote in his diary about a slave who regularly "pretended to be too heavy [pregnant] to work"[54] and another who managed to get eleven months of reduced work assignments because of an overlong pregnancy.

Occasionally, both male and female slaves rebelled violently, destroying equipment, burning down the plantation house, or even murdering their owners. In 1681 a woman and two men in Massachusetts attempted to burn down their master's home. In 1754 two female slaves set fire to their master's buildings in Charleston, South Carolina; the master responded by having them burned alive. A year later, a female house slave was burned at the stake in Charleston for poisoning her master, a dire warning to other house slaves. Women also participated in slave revolts, including those occurring on Long Island in 1708, New York City in 1712, and Louisiana in 1732.

Surviving the Slave System

With the advent of the American Revolution and the rhetoric of freedom ringing

Slaves were often whipped by plantation owners to puish them for running away.

in the ears of residents throughout the colonies, a growing number of colonists began to question the wisdom and integrity of slavery, but it would take almost another hundred years and much bloodshed before the institution of slavery would be abolished and the slaves set free.

Meanwhile, outnumbered and outgunned, the majority of slaves resigned themselves to their fate and made the most of their situation. As they worked in the fields and in the slave quarter, women shared their memories of Africa with each other and with their children. In the little free time they were allowed, they told stories, sang,

danced, and played whatever musical instruments they could fashion. In the process, they forged a new, unique African American community and culture. In the essay "Slave Songs and Slave Consciousness," historian Lawrence W. Levine writes, "Slaves often took over entire white hymns and folk songs, . . . but altered them significantly in terms of words, musical structure, and especially performance before making them their own. The result was a hybrid with a strong African base."[55]

In many regions of colonial America, the social networks of the slaves were strengthened by a cooperative spirit born

A Profamily Petition

By the end of the colonial era, the seeds of a movement for the abolition of slavery were beginning to take hold. In 1773 a group of African Americans argued before the Massachusetts legislature that slavery undermined Christian values. This excerpt from their testimony is from *America at 1750*, by Richard Hofstadter.

The enduring ties of husband and wife we are strangers to for we are no longer man and wife than our masters or mistresses thin, proper. . . . Our children are also taken from us by force and sent many miles from us where we seldom see them again. [They're] to be made slaves of for life which sometimes is very short by reason of being dragged from their mothers' breasts. How can a slave perform the duties of a husband to a wife or parent to his child? How can a husband leave master and work and cleave to his wife? How can the wife submit themselves to their husbands in all things? How can the child obey his parents in all things?

of living and working in such close quarters. Slaves could not look to laws to protect them in their dealings with one another; they were instead governed by their own set of rules. Carol Berkin writes, "Working collectively and cooperatively, slaves were able to carve out other autonomous realms. Slave midwives and slave doctors shaped the medical care of the quarter, and slave communities established their own burial and societies and burial rituals." [56]

Under the harsh conditions of slavery, the survival of the African slave is testimony to the survival of the human spirit. Hofstadter writes, "The Africans had endured the unendurable; they survived; they made for themselves such a life as life would allow them." [57]

Chapter 4:
Colonial Women in the Workforce

❧

Throughout the colonies, women played an important role in business affairs. The wives of modest farmers kept their families fed by selling or trading surplus produce or homemade goods. Wives of fishermen, artisans, and shopkeepers supported the work of their husbands by staffing their stores and selling their wares. Stephanie Grauman Wolf points out, "It required full-time employment—rarely achieved—by both husband and wife, and a year with no unforeseen disasters, for independent artisans in the lower crafts and unskilled laborers to cover the essentials of rent, firewood, food, and clothes for a family of five."[58]

Unmarried women, called *femes sole,* also became adept in a variety of occupations. Widows often took over their husbands' businesses, becoming innkeepers and shopkeepers, printers and newspaper publishers, butchers and bakers, even shoemakers and blacksmiths. Others owned and managed real estate, both large plantations and smaller parcels of land. As early as 1692, the Massachusetts legislature passed a law

stating that though unmarried women were to be considered their fathers' responsibility, this requirement should not "hinder any single woman of good repute for the exercise of any lawful trade or employment for a livelihood."[59]

New Influences

The British colonies at first patterned their laws on those of the mother country, including restrictions on the legal status of women. Married women could neither own property nor represent themselves in a court of law, for example. English custom also frowned on women owning shops or engaging in trade. These colonial social norms soon eroded, not only because colonial life required women to take on new roles but also because British settlers were influenced by people from places with more liberal or egalitarian views. The colonists in New Netherland (which became New York in 1664) had a different set of traditions from those in the British colonies concerning the rights of married women. Dutch women, married as well as single, could buy and sell goods and property, could contract debt, and could bring suits in a court of law. Wives had equal claim to the family's wealth and could decide who would inherit their money upon their death. Kamensky writes, "To the Dutch and their American-born descendants, marriage was like a business venture in which husbands were the senior partners while wives were prized junior executives."[60]

As a result, the Dutch colonies were home to many of America's first business-women. Margaret Hardenbroek, who emigrated from Holland to New Amsterdam (present-day New York City) in 1659, is famous for her entrepreneurial spirit and her business acumen. Upon arriving in the New World with her first husband, Peter De Vries, Hardenbroek began to trade, buying furs in the colonies and sending them to Holland in exchange for pins, cooking oil, and vinegar.

When De Vries died, Hardenbroek sold their property in Staten Island and invested it in ships, establishing what is

Ships sail into New York's harbor in this seventeenth-century illustration. Many of America's first businesswomen lived in New York and other colonies with a strong Dutch heritage.

believed to be the first packet line between Europe and America. Within two years of her husband's death, she married Frederick Philipsen, a carpenter-cum-trader, but she continued to conduct business under her maiden name. She also took care to protect her assets from Philipsen's control, a legal option that was unavailable to colonial women in the English colonies. Carol Berkin explains:

> By the terms of the traditional Dutch . . . marriage contract, Margaret preserved both her legal identity and her financial prerogatives, an arrangement as routine under Dutch law as it was unusual to seventeenth-century English marriage codes. [61]

The shrewd business sense and entrepreneurial spirit of Hardenbroek and Philipsen soon made them the richest couple in New Amsterdam.

Deputy Husbands

Informally, women throughout the colonies were expected to take on business responsibilities. In the English colonies, when a man was away, his wife took over the responsibility for both his home and his business. "Because wives remained close to the house," writes Laurel Thatcher Ulrich, "they were often at the communications center of these diverse [business] operations, given responsibility for conveying directions, pacifying creditors, and perhaps even making some decisions about the disposition of labor." [62]

And most men in colonial America had to travel at some point or another. Farmers went to market to sell their harvest and to town to buy supplies. Quakers and other missionaries traveled among Native Americans and nonbelievers to preach the faith. Fur traders spent weeks traveling back and forth from the frontier to the coast buying furs from Native American trappers and then selling them to ship owners bound for Europe. Southern plantation owners with far-flung properties often had to spend significant time traveling among them to make sure their business was running smoothly. And all along the eastern seaboard, merchants and fishermen were at sea for months, and sometimes years, at a time.

In the words of one seventeenth-century Englishman: A woman "in her husband's absence, is wife and deputy-husband, which makes her double the files of her diligence. At his return he finds all things so well he wonders to see himself at home when he was abroad." [63] As this observer points out, despite the need to do the work of two people, the "deputy-husband" often was so efficient that the actual husband's absence was not even apparent.

Women thus became well acquainted with their husbands' enterprises, familiarity that could be essential to a widow's very survival upon her husband's death. They also wielded considerable influence; many men sought their wives' opinion on everything from hiring and staffing needs to how they might best expand their business. Historian Carol Berkin explains how a wise woman could further the interests of all those involved in a transaction:

> Salem [Massachusetts] court records show a wife not only present during her husband's negotiation on the sale of a land and a house but "furthering the sale." Creditors suing their debtors called on their wives, who were "present at the bargain making," to corroborate their testimony. Women served as historians of their husbands' economic affairs, recalling under oath former ownership of property and its location as well as details of their neighbors' and kinsmen's finances. [64]

Pennsylvania printer Benjamin Franklin's wife, Deborah Read Franklin, took over her husband's business affairs, enabling him to work to secure the liberty of the colonies and to plan the government of the new United States. Benjamin Franklin noted to a friend in 1745 that marriage had become a necessity for the enterprising man: "It is the Man and Woman united that make the compleat human Being," he wrote. "Together they are likely to succeed in the World." [65]

Benjamin Franklin's wife, Deborah, managed his business affairs while he was away.

Businesswomen by Necessity

Many American women became adept businesswomen by necessity. Even those whose attention was focused primarily on traditionally feminine spheres of home and family were forced to engage in trade in order to survive and thrive in the economy of the New World. "Tending only to the upkeep of one's own home and the comfort of one's own family was a luxury afforded to comparatively few colonial women," writes Stephanie Grauman Wolf. "Farm wives not only supplemented the family income with the processed goods and 'truck' of their kitchen gardens and dairies, but also wove straw hats from Caribbean straw provided by local shopkeepers and baskets from reeds they found by the river." [66]

In fact, many farming women made the transition from an informal trading partnership of homespun products to a commercial enterprise. Author Sarah M. Evans writes that in Brandywine, Pennsylvania,

> farm women shifted their work from spinning and weaving to the production of butter. First they sold their surplus to exporters trading with the West Indies. Then as Philadelphia grew into a major city, they found a ready urban market. The income from women's butter production brought a new affluence to "middling" farm families, allowing women to buy goods they had previously produced themselves and sustaining the family economy in the face of rising costs. [67]

Single women and widows in urban areas had to find other ways to support themselves. Many did what they knew best and focused their attention on traditional female activities. They entered domestic servitude, becoming cooks, nannies, or washwomen for the growing number of wealthy families in colonial America's cities.

Others spun yarn or thread for cloth merchants or advertised their services as seamstresses.

Widows often took advantage of the one thing left to them by their husbands—their homes. Even a modest home, if well situated, could provide women with a living. Women rented out rooms by the month or night; they also provided meals to weary travelers. Elisabeth Anthony Dexter writes:

> These hostelries were of all types, from that of the woman who merely consented to rent a room and furnish meals on demand, to that of the hostess whose excellent tavern was known for miles around. There, travelers betook themselves gladly, the judges on circuit made a point of dining, and groups, such as proprietors of townships, held their regular meetings. [68]

Women also ran taverns and, later, coffee shops, which were quite popular in England in the mid-1700s. As early as 1647, a Mrs. Clark, a widow in Salem, Massachusetts, was granted a license to sell wine; in the 1650s, a woman was granted a license to operate a tavern in Northumberland County, Virginia. Records from Boston in 1714 reveal that twelve of Boston's thirty-four innkeepers and seventeen of forty-one liquor retailers were women.

Teachers and Tutors

Better-educated women offered their services as tutors, governesses, or teachers in one of the many "dame schools" that cropped up throughout rural America. The dame schools were led by one of the better-educated women of the community who conducted lessons for children in her kitchen or living room. Some of the founding fathers learned to read and write at these schools. Sarah Knight, a widow who opened a dame school in 1706 in Boston, counted Benjamin Franklin and Samuel Mather among her pupils.

Women also occasionally served as teachers in public elementary schools or opened private finishing schools where they taught French, painting, music, dance,

"The Ambiguous Position of Widows"

The roles of men and women in colonial America were complex, particularly in the case of unmarried women. In *Founding Mothers and Fathers,* Mary Beth Norton discusses the customs dictating the roles of the sexes and what she calls the "ambiguous position of widows."

Certainly, in some ways a widow was able to take her dead husband's place at the head of the family. Her position as sole household governor afforded her unquestioned primacy over her children and servants. If she took on the responsibility of administering her husband's estate, as was customary, she became liable for paying his debts. Unless she remarried, she could sue or be sued in her own name, make contracts, and draft a will.

In other important ways, though, a widow did not resemble a male household head, precisely because she was not a man. She assumed her husband's familial roles, but not most of his political responsibilities. Although she had to pay taxes, she could not vote, serve in the militia or on juries, or hold any sort of elective or appointive office. . . . Thus a widow's gender identity fundamentally affected her social, political, and economic roles, especially those beyond the confines of her household. She was simultaneously both female and male: female, in that like other women she was excluded from certain political and military obligations; male, in that like men she had economic responsibilities and automatic rule over her own household. . . . Colonial authorities vacillated in their dealings with widows, because . . . a widow's proper role was by no means clear.

A woman tutors children in her living room. Educated women of colonial America easily found work as tutors, teachers, or governesses.

embroidery, arts and crafts, or other skills thought to be of importance for a colonial lady. Widowed at just nineteen years of age, Sarah Haggar Wheaten of Newport, Rhode Island, developed her dame school into a successful boarding school; by 1758 she had more than seventy students. There were a growing number of finishing schools for young ladies in the South as well. In 1734 a woman known as the Widow Varnod opened a French school for girls in South Carolina; in 1754, Mary Salisbery advertised

a boarding school in Annapolis, Maryland, for girls who "wished to learn French and fancy needlework."[69]

Midwives and Medicine

Yet another occupation considered appropriate for women was midwifery. Midwives were highly skilled women who presided over almost all the births in the New World. Over the course of a midwife's lifetime, she might help deliver hundreds or even thousands of babies. Elizabeth Philips of Charles

Town, South Carolina; Catherine Blaikley of Williamsburg, Virginia; and a Mrs. Thomas Whitmore of Marlboro, Vermont, are each credited with assisting the birth of two to three thousand infants.

A forerunner of today's obstetrician, the midwife encountered a range of complications, from breach babies to premature births. The skill of midwives was not lost on the colonial population. "The position of the midwife was secure and respected," writes Stephanie Grauman Wolf. "She was regarded as a professional to be paid for her ministrations, consulted during pregnancy, totally in charge in the delivery room and usually able to overrule husbands who tried to interfere."[70] Furthermore, in an era in which women usually lacked the right to testify in court, midwives regularly served as expert witnesses in cases involving doubtful pregnancy or potential infanticide.

In addition to delivering babies, many of these midwives served as nurses to the general population. The 1739 obituary notice of Mary Hazard of Newport, Rhode Island, (who died at ninety-nine), calls her "a very useful gentlewoman, both to poor and rich, and particularly among sick persons for her skill and judgment, which she did gratis [free of charge]."[71]

With the rise of professional doctors, women began to collect fees for their services as doctors or nurses. Anne Mountfort Eliot served as a doctor in Roxbury, Massachusetts, in the 1660s; Elizabeth King practiced medicine in Southold, Long Island, a century later; and Susanna Wright, a Quaker, served as the community physician in Lancaster, Pennsylvania, for several decades. Women also nursed sick and wounded soldiers throughout the colonial period. During the French and Indian War and the American Revolution, nurses accompanied the troops into battle. They not only cared for the sick and wounded, but did much of the cooking and laundering as well.

Craftswomen and Artists

As a colonial upper class emerged, educated women who enjoyed leisure time began to sculpt, paint, and write. Many confined themselves to "women's arts," expressing their creativity in needlecraft, quilts, or furniture decoration. But others moved into less traditionally feminine spheres. In the early eighteenth century, more than forty of the local officials and well-to-do citizens in Charles Town, South Carolina, commissioned Henrietta Johnston for portraits. In 1734, Mary Roberts advertised portraits in the *South Carolina Gazette;* in 1772, a Miss Reid offered to do pastel portraits.

Women sometimes engaged in occupations that even today are considered male dominated. They became barbers and morticians, blacksmiths and upholsterers. Mary Salmon of Boston continued her late husband's horseshoeing business; Mary

Crowley of Philadelphia took over her husband's tanning shop; Elizabeth Russell of Quaker City, Pennsylvania, a coach-making enterprise; Sarah Jewell, a rope-making business. And in 1772, Massachusetts widow Anna Jones announced in the local newspaper that she would be taking over her husband's distillery.

A significant number of women could also be found among the colonial printers and publishers. After the death of her husband in 1695, Dinah Nuthead, the illiterate wife of a Maryland printer, took over her husband's business. She did so well that

Some colonial women entered the publishing business and operated printing presses like this one.

the Maryland legislature hired her as its official printer.

Dinah Nuthead is believed to be the first female American printer, but she was followed by many others. Despite the fact that newspaper printing was difficult work, requiring the type for each letter and word to be set by hand, a number of women were found among the ranks of colonial printers. While John Peter Zenger was serving a sentence for libel in 1734–1735, his wife, Anna, kept the presses running at the *New York Weekly Journal.* Widowed eleven years later, Anna Zenger once more took over the enterprise.

Elizabeth Timothy of South Carolina also took over her husband's publication upon his death. For ten years, she painstakingly ensured that the *Gazette,* South Carolina's first permanent newspaper, came out twice a week. Zenger and Timothy both left their businesses to their sons when the young men were old enough to take over, but the women's success can be measured in the wealth they acquired. When Elizabeth Timothy died in 1757, her worldly possessions included three houses, a large piece of land, and eight slaves.

"She-Merchants"

Finally, women made money as merchants of a wide range of commodities, from gourmet foods to fine wines to pharmaceuticals, from farm equipment to metal tools and even firearms. The first woman shopkeeper on record was a Mrs. Goose

Most colonial women worked in or near their homes; rarely did women work as part of a larger labor force in colonial America. By the middle of the eighteenth century, however, a few entrepreneurs tried to capture the power of the female workforce by hiring them as employees in large textile companies. In *As Various as Their Land,* Stephanie Grauman Wolf concludes, "All failed largely because even very poor women could not bring themselves to toil for so little money in such an unfamiliar and uncongenial environment."

In Philadelphia, the Friends of American Manufacturers organization fared better by employing men to work at weaving equipment in the factory and employing women to spin at home. Company agents distributed flax to hundreds of urban women who were then paid when they returned with yarn that met the company standards of quality. By allowing women to continue to work at home, as they had always done, this arrangement integrated age-old customs and roles and an emerging manufacturing economy.

of Salem, Massachusetts, who sold groceries in 1643. Most shops in the early colonial period sold dry goods and household items such as soap, sugar, spices, and other necessities.

Shopkeeping rarely provided the sole means of livelihood; rather, most shopkeepers sold wares in addition to farming, bar- or innkeeping, or craftsmanship. Artisans often employed their wives (or children or servants) to staff small stores where they worked. Hannah Grafton, a mariner's wife in Salem, Massachusetts, had a shop attached to her house where she sold everything from hardware and tools to imported cloth and sewing supplies.

The number of women shopkeepers and tradespersons continued to grow throughout the colonial period. In her landmark book *Colonial Women of Affairs,* Elisabeth Anthony Dexter estimated that women accounted for 9.5 percent of Boston's merchants in 1773. By this time, the variety of goods that could be purchased in the average colonial city seemed infinite. Some shops catered to the growing upper class with exotic, expensive, and purely decorative items. In 1751, Elizabeth Murray advertised that she would sell all kinds of material, hats of the newest fashion, jewelry, women's shoes, stockings, gloves, and needles and thread. Another she-merchant, known only as Mrs. Samuel Bourdet, advertised that she carried "a complete line of European finery"; she also catered to male customers by including among her wares "saws, firearms, and hinges."[72] Those who were adept seamstresses also might sell ready-to-wear garments, such as Mary Cahell of Philadelphia, who advertised

> all sorts of gentlemens caps, Leather, etc. Also ladies and childrens caps, mantilets, pillareens, hoods, bonnets, long and short cloaks, mantles, and scarfs; with black bags and roses for gentlemens hair or wigs; all which she makes after the newest and neatest fashions, very cheap. N.B. She makes turbans for Negroes.[73]

Competition was fierce, and profits could dwindle quickly for any number of reasons. Shortages could result from shipping delays or bad weather; a sudden surplus of goods when more than one shipment came in at once could drive down demand for and prices of highly sought-after goods; a bad harvest could cause a sudden collapse in the local economy. As towns grew, however, selling wares from Europe and other places became a lucrative enterprise for some entrepreneurial men and women. An Ipswich, Massachusetts, woman known only as Mistress Hewlett became so successful in the poultry business that her husband asked her for a loan.

Women of Property

In addition to going into business, women made money on land. Selma R. Williams concludes, "In all colonies, the single woman's most notable achievement in business outside the home was land management."[74]

As executor of their husbands' estate, widows sometimes supported themselves by leasing out small tracts of land or rental properties. For over twenty years in the mid–eighteenth century, Sarah Boylston of Boston advertised property to rent. Although many colonists assumed that women would be easy targets for unscrupulous businessmen, female landowners usually boldly carried out their responsibilities. Elizabeth Powel, the widow of Samuel Powel, a wealthy man who had served as the mayor of Philadelphia, once lectured a tenant who was delinquent in his rent, saying, "[as a] Man of business [I] must be sensible that if I wish to preserve integrity in my own engagements I take care that others are punctual in their payments to me."[75]

It was not uncommon for a widow to take over her husband's house or farm, but a few women managed significant acreage. Cornelia Shuyler, a wealthy Dutchwoman of New Amsterdam, had at one time over thirteen hundred acres. And Margaret Brent, who immigrated to Maryland in the seventeenth century, increased her small land grant to well over a thousand acres, becoming one of the most influential landowners in Maryland and one of the wealthiest women in all of the colonies.

Under the laws of most of the colonies, women could not own land outright. Some colonies made an effort to protect a married woman's interest in the land by requiring her consent before her husband could sell real estate. Others made provisions for widows to use the land upon their husbands' death. Under most inheritance laws, however, ownership of land was to pass to sons. However, many property owners, especially planters with ample land, remembered in their wills their daughters, especially unmarried daughters. In the first two decades of the eighteenth century,

for example, two-thirds of the Baltimore County men with estates of four hundred acres gave land to their daughters.

Women who inherited land had much to learn because the plantations of the South were complex businesses. Owners were responsible for hundreds of acres, a reluctant (and often hostile) workforce, and crops that required attention year-round. Managing a plantation required making sure that crops were planted at the right time of year and on land that was suitably fertile. In addition to running the manor house and taking care of the cooking, washing, and feeding of her family and laborers, the plantation mistress often assumed some responsibilities for the fields. Plantation

A Petition to Be Heard

In 1733 a loose coalition of widows, many of whom were businesswomen in New York, went beyond what many believed to be proper for women by issuing a petition requesting a voice in official politics. "We the widows of this city, have had a Meeting, and . . . our case is something Deplorable," they wrote, asking editor John Peter Zenger to publish their petition. Zenger duly published the following in the *Weekly Journal*. It is reprinted in Sarah M. Evans's *Born for Liberty*:

We are House keepers, Pay our Taxes, carry on Trade, and most of us are she Merchants, and as we in some measure contribute to the Support of Government, we ought to be Intitled to some of the Sweets of it; but we find ourselves entirely neglected, while the Husbands that live in our Neighborhood are daily invited to Dine at Court; we have the Vanity to think we can be full as Entertaining, and make as brave a Defense in Case of an Invasion and perhaps not turn Tail so Soon as some of them.

wives oversaw the business when their husbands were away and might take over entirely after being widowed. Upon being widowed in the 1690s, Elizabeth Digges took on responsibility for her husband's tobacco plantation and their 108 slaves, the most in all of Virginia. Similarly, when her husband died shortly after arriving in South Carolina, Rebecca Axtell organized the plantation so well that in 1705 she was given a grant of an additional thousand acres.

Eliza Pinckney: Plantation Mistress

The most famous female plantation owner was Eliza Lucas Pinckney. Born on the sugar island of Antigua in 1722 to a wealthy planter, Eliza lived the life of an aristocrat. She was sent to London to receive an education and was fluent in French, well read in the literature of the day, accomplished in music, and skilled in needlepoint. At sixteen, Eliza moved with her father to a plantation in South Carolina. When her father was forced to leave soon thereafter, he left Eliza behind to manage his three plantations in South Carolina: Wappoo, the plantation on which Eliza and her family lived, covered six hundred acres; the others, fifteen hundred acres and three thousand acres. "I have the business of three plantations to transact," Eliza wrote to a friend in May 1740. "[The enterprise] requires much

writing and more business and fatigue of other sorts than you can imagine."[76]

But Eliza proved equal to the task. She introduced a variety of new crops to the plantation, experimenting with ginger, cotton, and figs. When she tried indigo, a plant yielding a deep blue dye, she hit on a winner. Indigo soon became one of the region's most profitable export crops. Eliza wrote to her father in 1744, "We please ourselves with the prospect of exporting in a few years a good quantity of [indigo] from hence, and supplying our Mother Country with a manufacture for which she has so great a demand, and which she is now supplied with from the French colonies and many thousands pounds per annum thereby lost to the nation."[77]

In 1744, Eliza married Charles Pinckney, a close family friend and prominent lawyer. With Charles frequently away on business in Charleston, she continued managing the plantations and experimenting with new crops.

Science and Invention

Eliza Pinckney was not the only woman in colonial America to experiment with new crops. Martha Logan, who lived on a large plantation in Charles Town, South Carolina, was a well-known horticulturist. Author of *The Gardener's Calendar*, Logan also operated a nursery and sold seeds for vegetables, flowers, and fruit trees.

New Yorker Jane Colden distinguished herself as a botanist. In 1757 she produced a catalog fully describing more than three hundred local plant species. "She has discovered a great number of plants never before described," wrote a contemporary Scottish botanist, "and has given them properties and virtues, many of which are found useful in medicine, and she draws and colors them with great beauty."[78]

Colonial America was open to new ideas, and women rose to the challenge of finding new ways to get the work done. In the early 1700s, Sibylla Masters, a Quaker in Philadelphia, developed an innovative method of pulverizing corn into meal. In 1715 she received a patent for her invention, which relied on stamping the corn rather than grinding it. She also came up with a special process for weaving straw, and proceeded to make and market bonnets, baskets, and chairs using the new weaving method.

Overcoming the Odds

Regardless of the type of business, women faced many obstacles to success. Most women in colonial America were unschooled. They lacked basic bookkeeping skills and often had to hire someone to figure their accounts. Married women were also hampered by laws that did not allow them to sue creditors or make contracts. Any money that a woman earned was subject to her husband's control. This might not matter much for women who were happily married, but could be devastating for those in unhappy marriages.

The difficulties are evident in one story of a young Virginia woman named Susannah Cooper. In 1720 Susannah's husband left her. In just three years of marriage, her husband had not only spent Susannah's substantial dowry but racked up a mountain of debts. Because she was still technically married, Susannah Cooper could not sell any assets or sue those who owed her money. Recognizing the injustice of the situation, the Virginia legislature passed a private bill giving her the status of *feme sole,* or single woman.

Against all odds, colonial women of all classes and in all regions proved that they could and would succeed in forging a new life for themselves. On their own and married, woman after woman proved her ability to survive and succeed by using the assets and skills they had—a well-located home, a skill in sewing or spinning, a basic knowledge of childbirth and healing, a knack for knowing what people wanted or needed, or simple intelligence and business acumen.

Chapter 5:
Church and Community Leaders

The women of colonial America formed a network of relationships with one another. They came together to work and to trade. They supported one another during childbirth and other critical life events. They also came together to practice their religion. Pious women met weekly, or even daily, to read the Bible and to pray. Church-sponsored groups of women helped the needy and the poor. In some sects—most notably the Quakers—the church gave women power over the woman's domain, putting experienced matrons in charge of making sure younger women adhered to the societal customs of the day. But even among the strict Puritans, who believed in the subordination and submission of women, colonial women found a way to make their voices heard.

Life in Puritan New England

The Puritans had come to the New World to forge a new and better way of life in the practice of a strict faith. They sought to live in adherence to what they understood as God's laws. John Winthrop, the Puritan leader of the Massachusetts Bay Colony, declared that theirs was a mission "to do justly, to love mercy, to walk humbly with our God." He further set his sights on establishing "a city upon a hill" [79] that would serve as an example for the world to follow. He and his contemporaries in communities throughout New England set out to create communities that followed God's commandments. The Puritan leaders served as magistrates and legislators of the community, determining the laws to be upheld and enforcing these laws.

From the beginning, the Puritan leaders required people to obey biblical principles and the laws they based on these principles. The Sabbath was strictly observed. Puritans were expected to spend most of their Sundays in church, and the courts regularly punished those who stayed away. The Sabbath law forbade people not only work, but simple pleasures such as visiting or picnicking. Mortal sins like adultery and blasphemy were punishable by death.

The Puritans also had strict rules about the appropriate role of women in society.

Women and men entered church through separate doors and sat apart from one another in the pews. Women were not allowed to hold office in the Puritan church. They also were denied access to taverns, courtrooms, and most other public places. Puritan goodwives, as they were called, were expected to obey their husbands.

For the most part, the people who settled in the Puritan communities of New England wanted to follow the strict laws that were written, for they too wanted to live a godly life. After all, this was the goal of the waves of English settlers who crossed the Atlantic Ocean during the seventeenth century.

Most Puritan women believed wholeheartedly in the Scriptures and took religion very seriously. Leading a Christian life was something to strive for, and the rewards were the riches of heaven. The women of seventeenth-century New England read the Bible and meditated on its meaning. Puritan women often gathered together at the home of a respected woman for informal prayer and meditation. They attended church each Sunday and listened with rapt attention. The sermons often addressed the nature of women and what preachers considered the natural duties of men and women.

Membership in a church provided Puritan women with a more public role than their other activities. Going to church meant getting out into the community,

away from the ever-demanding duties of housewifery. Church membership also allowed a woman a separate identity from her husband. Historian Laurel Thatcher Ulrich writes, "A woman could be admitted to the Table of the Lord [church communion] regardless of the status, economic position, or religious proclivities of her husband. . . . With or without his blessing, she could settle accounts with God." [80]

Women also played an important role in deciding how to deal with charity cases. The 1648 document that governed the churches of Massachusetts Bay had decreed, "The Lord hath appointed ancient widows, where they may be had, to minister in the Church, in giving attendance to the sick, and to give succour unto them and others in the like necessities." [81] As a result, prominent widows were occasionally tapped to serve as church deacons, with the general responsibility of helping the poor and sick members of the congregation. Contemporary writings laud the Puritan women for the charity work they did in connection with the church.

The Complex Relationship of Church and Community

By the mid–seventeenth century, women outnumbered men in most churches, and more than three-quarters of the membership of some congregations was female. As women's numbers in the church grew, so did their informal influence. Furthermore, because the affairs of the church and of the community were inextricable in Puritan communities, as women gained influence over church affairs, they had an effect on town politics as well. As members of the church, women were allowed to participate in discussions of issues of local importance, such as whether to build new roads or schools and whether taxes should be increased. Women could not vote on such issues, but they sometimes wielded significant influence nonetheless.

Building a new church was a particularly thorny issue. Hampered by pregnancy and small children, women on the periphery of town began to put pressure on their husbands to establish a new church. Ulrich writes, "Men signed the petitions, wrote the appeals, and cast the votes, but women frequently supplied the energy which established new congregations and parishes in the outlying areas of older towns." [82]

Because churches were tax-supported public institutions, decisions regarding whether and where to build a new church often had economic and political consequences. Men sometimes debated such issues for months. On at least one occasion, women decided not to wait for their decision. In 1677 residents of Chebacco, a settlement over three miles from Ipswich, Massachusetts, petitioned the town of

Like this young couple, people on the outskirts of town often had to walk several miles to and from church.

Ipswich for permission to hire a minister so that they could avoid the long journey to church each Sunday. In a church history, the parish clerk writes of the role of women in the Chebacco church's founding: "While

Anne Hutchinson

❧

Anne Hutchinson was born Anne Marbury in 1591 in Alford, England. The daughter of a clergyman, Anne grew up among books and religious discussions. In 1612 she married William Hutchinson, a merchant, with whom she had fourteen children. Anne Hutchinson and her family migrated to the Massachusetts Bay Colony in 1634, settling in that colony's largest city, Boston.

Hutchinson soon gained respect and renown among her neighbors. She began to organize weekly meetings of Boston women to discuss recent sermons and advance her own controversial theological views. Hutchinson stressed that people could have a relationship with God without observing institutionalized beliefs and their ministers, which Puritan leaders viewed as attacks on their strict moral and legal codes and on the authority of the Massachusetts clergy.

When John Winthrop was elected governor of Massachusetts Bay, Hutchinson's support among the political leadership began to erode. In 1637 she was tried by the General Court of Massachusetts, presided over by Governor John Winthrop, on the charge of heresy. Hutchinson was found guilty, excommunicated from the Boston church, and banished from the colony.

Eight months pregnant with her fifteenth child, Hutchinson moved with her husband, family, and a small group of followers to the island of Aquidneck (now part of Rhode Island). After the death of her husband, she moved with her family to a frontier settlement on Long Island. In 1643 Hutchinson and all but one member of her family were killed when their new home was attacked by Native Americans. Hearing of the tragedy, some of the Puritan faithful cited the attack on Hutchinson and her family a manifestation of divine judgment.

we were in this great conflict that all things seemed to act against us some women without the knowledge of their husbands and with the advice of some few men went to other towns and got help and raised the house that we intended for a meeting house if we could git liberty [permission to hire a minister]."[83]

Radical Ideas: The Tale of Anne Hutchinson

The Chebacco women's initiative was a rare exception, however. Pious Puritans, as in most other churches in colonial America, were expected to heed Saint Paul's admonition: "Let the woman learn in silence with all subjection. But I suffer not a woman to teach, nor to usurp authority over the man, but to be in silence" (I Tim. 2:11–12). Virtuous women might play an important role within the family or group of close associates, but they were expected to be students and not teachers in religious matters.

The most famous woman to test these assumptions was Anne Hutchinson. Hutchinson immigrated to Boston in 1634 and, according to historians Flexner and Fitzpatrick, soon became respected throughout the community for "her rare knowledge of healing herbs, and . . . her eloquence."[84] Soon after her arrival in Boston, Anne Hutchinson began hosting Bible meetings in her home.

At first, the Puritan leaders approved of Hutchinson's meetings, but they soon changed their minds. Over time, the weekly meetings grew; by 1636, sixty to eighty people came from miles around to hear her speak. Most of Hutchinson's adherents were women, but many prominent men attended as well, including Harry Vane, governor of the colony; John Wheelwright, her brother-in-law and a Puritan minister; William Coddington, a magistrate of Boston; and John Cotton, a well-respected leader of the church.

It soon became clear that Hutchinson's meetings were no ordinary prayer meetings. Hutchinson was interpreting the Bible, something that only men were supposed to do. Hutchinson also criticized some of the Puritan leaders, who, she said, emphasized "works" (the appearance of doing good) over faith. She called on pious men and women to challenge their ministers and to seek direct communication with God.

John Winthrop and other Puritan leaders fought back. Hugh Peter, the minister of Hutchinson's church in Salem, admonished Hutchinson before the congregation. "You have stepped out of your place," he said,

Accused of heresy, Anne Hutchinson stands before Puritan leader John Winthrop.

"you have rather been a Husband than a Wife and a preacher than a Hearer; and a Magistrate than a Subject."[85] Charged with "trouble[ing] the peace of the commonwealth and the churches here,"[86] Hutchinson was banished from Massachusetts.

Hundreds of women came to the aid of Hutchinson, and families followed her to Rhode Island, where several people cast out from Massachusetts Bay had already settled. Even Margaret Winthrop, the wife of John Winthrop, who led the Puritan community in which Hutchinson was tried for treason, was not convinced that her husband had made a wise decision. She wrote in a letter to husband John about Hutchinson:

> Sad thoughts possess my spirits, and I cannot repulse them; which makes me unfit for anything, wondering what the Lord means by all these troubles among us. Sure I am that all shall work to the best to them that love God, or rather are loved of him. I know He will bring light out of obscurity and make his righteousness shine forth as clear as the noonday. Yet I find in myself an adverse spirit, and a trembling heart, not so willing to submit to the will of God as I desire.[87]

Witches and Witchcraft

Strong religious leaders like Anne Hutchinson were not the only women who alarmed Puritan men. They also feared that women would take power as witches. The Puritans believed witches existed, just as they believed the devil existed and could direct human behavior and cause human misery. They sometimes pointed to witchcraft as the cause of any number of unexplainable mysteries. For example, witches were accused of damaging crops and destroying property, of spreading illness and disease, of causing deformities in newborns.

Accusations of witchcraft did not originate in the colonies; witch trials had taken place in England for hundreds of years. Nor was Salem, Massachusetts, the first place in the colonies to witness the malevolence of witchcraft; witches had been put to death in several other colonies. However, nowhere has the scope and intensity of witch trials matched what occurred in Salem in 1692.

The Salem witch trials began in January of that year, when the nine-year-old daughter and twelve-year-old niece of Reverend Samuel Parris of Salem Village began to suffer from seizures. When no medical explanation could be found, the Puritans turned to another explanation: bewitchment. Prodded by Parris and others, the girls described being "most greviously tortor[ed]"[88] and fingered their tormentors: Sarah Good, an impoverished widow who had previously been suspected of witchcraft; Sarah Osburn, an elderly woman who had been a newcomer to the village; and Tituba, a house servant. (Tituba is

The Power of Gossip

❧

In colonial America, men controlled the government and courtrooms, but women wielded significant influence through informal networks. Gossip and other informal means of sharing information were particularly important in communities in which there were no newspapers, which characterized most communities in seventeenth-century America. In the following excerpt from *Founding Mothers and Fathers,* Mary Beth Norton explains the role of gossip in colonial America.

> Reputations were sustained and lost in the early colonies primarily through gossip. The "brabling women," "Idle and busy headed people," and practitioners of "tale bearing or back biteing" targeted in Anglo-American slander statutes in fact served an important social function. Their gossip identified misbehavior and singled out misbehavers for community attention. The constant talk alerted colonists to potential problems in their daily interactions with others by raising questions about trustworthiness, sexual conduct, and less-than-admirable aspects of people's lives. In other words, gossip, for all its negative connotations, was a crucial mechanism of social control—one used by ordinary people themselves, and especially by women, who lacked men's easy access to courtrooms and other forums of the formal public. Married women in particular might be prohibited from taking independent legal action to protect their interests, but no law prevented a woman, whatever her marital status, from *talking* about a fellow colonist. Gossip was thus above all a woman's weapon, although men too employed it. Women were both major wielders of gossip and its frequent targets.

referred to in the records as an "Indian," but her origin is unknown. Many historians believe that she was from the West Indies.)

The accusations set off a cataclysmic chain of events. By the end of the summer, at least 144 people in the town of Salem and surrounding towns were arrested. Most were jailed for long periods of time; 3 women and a man died in custody. By the end 54 people had confessed to witchcraft. Nineteen were hanged and another man was pressed to death with heavy stones.

Women were at the center of the spectacle. Some historians believe that the Salem witch trials were, in fact, a response to the growing threat women posed to the existing social order. "As in no other event in American history until the rise of the women's rights movement in the nineteenth century, women took center stage at Salem," writes historian Mary Beth Norton. "They were the major instigators and victims of a remarkable public spectacle."[89]

The one role women were denied, of course, was as judge or jury. The judges and magistrates who decided the validity of the accusation and determined the fate of the accused were all men. Those who were convicted of witchcraft pled for mercy, often eloquently expressing the wrongs that were being committed. Before her hanging on September 19, Mary Easty, the sister of one of the "witches" who was hung in July, wrote in a petition to the magistrates and ministers:

> I know I must die, and my appointed time is set. But the Lord He knows it is, if it be possible, that no more innocent blood be shed, which undoubtedly cannot be avoided in the way and course you go in. I question not but your honors to do the utmost of your powers in the discovery and detecting of witchcraft and witches, and would not be guilty of innocent blood for the world. But by my own innocency I know you are in the wrong way.

In this fanciful depiction, a witch displays her powers at her trial in Salem. The Puritans strongly believed in the existence of witches.

The Lord in his infinite mercy direct you in this great work, if it be His blessed will, that innocent blood be not shed. [90]

Easty's fervent cry for justice was heard. Many people began to believe that the trials were claiming innocent lives. Less than a month after Easty was hung, Governor Phips suspended the arrest of suspected witches and further action against those already accused. The fury of the Salem witch-hunt subsided.

The Quakers

While Puritan women struggled to achieve strict obedience to male authorities, the Quakers offered more latitude to spiritual women. Like the Puritans before them, many Quakers traveled across the Atlantic Ocean from England to escape religious persecution in England and to establish a better way of life. Many settled along the banks of the Delaware River, where in 1681, the Society of Friends, as the Quakers were officially known, established what they called a Holy Experiment.

Women played a leading role in this experiment. The first wave of fifty-nine Quaker preachers who crossed the Atlantic between 1656 and 1663 included twenty-six women. In addition to becoming ordained, Quaker women served in other official capacities within the church and were encouraged to attend quarterly business sessions.

Quaker women and men were organized separately in the church hierarchy. Each group held a monthly meeting in which they discussed and decided on issues related to governing the local community. Quaker founders had intended that the women's meetings would serve as a training ground for Quaker wives and mothers, a place where women could serve as mentors and advisers. The goal of having women meet separately was, in fact, to encourage them to play a role in the discussions. "Why should women meet apart?" asked William Penn rhetorically in a 1692 pamphlet. "For a very good reason ... women whose bashfulness will not permit them to say or do much, as to church affairs before men, when by themselves, may exercise their gift of wisdom and understanding." [91]

At the men's meetings, members settled such issues as how to deal with a growing population and where to build new roads. Women, meanwhile, were charged with tasks related to the discipline of female members and taking care of the poor and needy. The women also were responsible for approving (or disallowing) marriages among church members. "The women's meetings had no authority to debate the larger, public issues, but they were far from ceremonial or social auxiliaries," Carol Berkin explains. "The women's meeting concerned itself exclusively with intra-community affairs, but in handling such matters, they were an autonomous and self-governing body."[92]

The women's meetings were led by respected matrons of the community, who also took it upon themselves to enforce the discipline of the sect. They policed their own sex with regard to dress, deportment, and speech, leading by example but not shying away from chastising others when necessary. The women usually assumed leadership positions in their thirties and tended to hold onto their leadership positions for several decades. One historian writes that Quaker matron Martha Thomas spent over three decades "traveling the Pennsylvania countryside to investigate, expose, condemn, and punish 'carnal talk' among female Friends"[93]

Quaker Missionaries

Throughout the seventeenth and eighteenth centuries, Quaker men and women became ministers and missionaries. They traveled and lived among Native Americans to teach them to read and write and to spread the gospel. As the Native Americans' traditional ways of life eroded, the Quakers also tried to teach them new ways to farm.

Quakers gather on their way to church. Unlike Puritan women, Quaker women served in official capacities in their churches.

Quakers also sought to liberate their white peers from Puritanism, which they viewed as an oppressive religion. Mary Dyer paid for these efforts with her life.

Mary Dyer was a colleague of Anne Hutchinson who followed Hutchinson to Rhode Island. In 1650, on a trip to England, Dyer and her husband became Quakers. Upon their return in 1657, Mary Dyer traveled to Massachusetts to meet with old friends and share her version of the word of God. She was imprisoned, released, and banished from the colony, the first of many times. Dyer defied the court by returning to Massachusetts repeatedly, even though defying banishment was a crime punishable by death. On October 19, 1659, the court sentenced Dyer to be hanged, but her sentence was overturned, and she was banished once again. When she was again brought before the Massachusetts courts in May 1660 for refusing to stay clear of the colony, the court sentenced Dyer to be executed and sent her to the gallows the very next day.

Community Leaders

While some Quakers were drawn to Massachusetts, others fled the harshness of Puritan rule. In 1642, Lady Deborah Moody was excommunicated by the Salem church for her radical opinions. Historians speculate that her wealth kept her from being banished by that community: Her four hundred acres of land in Salem and her farm on the outskirts of town generated considerable tax money for the colony. Although she was spared banishment, Moody voluntarily left Salem for New Netherland, where views tended to be more liberal. In 1645 she received a town charter from the Dutch government—becoming the first woman in the New World with such a charter—and founded the settlement of Gravesend on an uninhabited stretch of land that is present-day Long Island. Among the provisions of the Gravesend town patent was the protection of town residents to practice whatever religion they chose. Williams writes, "Here, her rebelliousness burst out in all directions. She refused to have a minister in her jurisdictions, or to keep the Sabbath, or to allow baptism of infants."[94] Quakers, Jews, and other religious outcasts were welcomed in Gravesend.

Like male leaders, Moody set about creating an ideal community. Under her direction, a unique plan for the town of Gravesend was laid out. The inhabited part of the town consisted of four squares of a little more than four acres each with ten house lots surrounding a one-acre commons. Radiating out from the center of the village were triangular one-hundred-acre farms, called boweries. "Gravesend was the only permanent settlement in America's early colonization period to have been initiated, planned, and directed by a woman," writes Thomas J. Campanella in *Landscape Journal*. "In its elegant and logical simplicity, the plan of Gravesend was almost without precedent in the English New World."[95]

Moody continued in her role as "Grand Dame of Gravesend" until her death at age seventy-three. She instituted regular town meetings at which townspeople could express their opinions on any number of public matters. Political leaders, including the governor, often consulted her on political matters. The governor sought her input on political nominations of magistrates; there is even a record of her voting in a colonywide election in 1655.

Another local community leader was Mary Coffin Starbuck, who lived on the fishing island of Nantucket, Massachusetts, at the turn of the eighteenth century. An esteemed Quaker preacher, Starbuck was sought after not only for her knowledge of opinion in matters of religion, but for her input on issues of town politics. Public business was often transacted at the Starbucks' home. Mary Starbuck's influence seems to have overshadowed that of her husband, a local official. John Richard, an Englishman who visited Nantucket in 1701, wrote of Mary Starbuck: "The islanders esteemed her as a judge among them, for little was done without her, as I understood. . . . She so far exceeded [her husband] in soundness of judgment, clearness of understanding, and an elegant way of expressing herself."[96]

The Religious Spectrum of Colonial America

The Puritans and Quakers were two prominent religious communities in colonial America, but many other sects played important roles in the lives of women. In the missions of New France, for example, Catholic women followed God's call to serve as missionaries, living among the Native Americans in an attempt to "civilize" them and convert them to Christianity. Marie Guyart, for example, left a convent in France for Quebec, where she spent over forty years as a teacher and mentor. Among her accomplishments were the establishment of a school for native children and the compilation of a French-Algonquian dictionary.

In the Anglican Church—the Church of England—a few women went beyond the conventions of the day that required women to be quiet, pious models of virtuousness. Mary Taney, for example, the wife of the sheriff of Calvert County, Maryland, lamenting the lack of parishioners in her community, petitioned the Church of England for funds to build a church there and retain a minister.

The first Methodist church organized in the New World was also inspired by a woman. In 1766, Barbara Ruckle Heck, who had become a Methodist in 1753, happened upon her brother and some friends playing cards. She threw the cards into the fire and warned the players that such foolishness presented a danger to the spirit. She then hurried to the house of her cousin, exclaiming, "Brother Embury, you must preach to us, or we shall all go to hell."[97] When her cousin declared that he could not preach because he had neither a congregation nor a meeting place, she invited him to her house to speak to a gathering of four.

From this inauspicious beginning, the Methodist congregation grew and was soon large enough to need a building. Heck declared that she had been praying on this matter for some time and "had received the assurance of the Lord's help in the undertaking."[98] She presented an architectural plan, which was readily approved, and did much of the work on the building herself.

As people traveled throughout the colonies and the world, they brought their religions with them. By the advent of the American Revolution, there were significant congregations of Anglicans, Dutch Reformed, Lutherans, Catholics, Methodists, and a host of other denominations. The slaves taken from Africa also added their varied religions to the mix.

In all of these sects, with the notable exception of the Quakers, women were expected to be subordinate. Carl Holliday writes, "In the Episcopal church of Virginia and the Carolinas, the Catholic Church of Maryland and Louisiana, and the Dutch church of New York, women were quiet onlookers, pious, reverent, and meek, freely acknowledging God in their lives, content to be seen and not heard."[99] It was women who filled the church pews of colonial America, but men who held the power.

Chapter 6:
Taking a Stand: Colonial Women as Political Activists

Throughout the colonial period of American history, women were denied a voice in political affairs. Single women and widows had to pay taxes, but usually could not vote or hold government office of any sort. They were not allowed to serve on juries or in the militia. Most colonies did not allow married women to represent themselves in a court of law or enter into contracts. Speaking in public or discussing politics in the privacy of one's home was considered unladylike. Politics was considered a dirty business, better left to men.

Unfit for Politics

In part, women were kept out of politics as part of the belief that they were unfit intellectually. American girls were given only a basic education. They were taught to read, mostly so they could read the Bible and pass on its teachings to their children. They also learned the skills they would need as mothers and wives—cooking, sewing, and the like—and perhaps gained basic musical and artistic training. But women were thought to be incapable of understanding politics, mathematics, science, or other "higher" subjects. "Why exclude women [from the vote]?" asked politician John Adams rhetorically in a letter to a colleague. "Because their delicacy renders them unfit for practice and experience in the great businesses of life, and the hardy enterprises of war. . . . Besides, their attention is so much engaged with the necessary nurture of their children, that nature has made them fittest for domestic cares." [100]

Some women believed that they were as capable as men, or could be given the opportunity. Judith Murray, for example, the daughter of a prosperous sea captain and merchant in Gloucester, Massachusetts, argued that it was the lack of education that resulted in a woman's inferiority: "It may be questioned, from what source doth this superiority [of males] . . . ? May we not trace its source in the difference of education and continued advantages? Will it be said that the judgment of a male two years old is more sage than that of a female's of the same age? I believe the reverse is generally observed to be true." [101] Despite the lack of education afforded to most colonial women, there were many examples of women who proved that they were every bit as capable as men.

Sarah Knight flouted the conventions that forbade a lady to travel alone and made a five-month journey from her home in Boston to New York and back. In the detailed journal of her observations, she demonstrates good humor and a keen sense of the workings of the world around her. "She demonstrates a profound political awareness, an understanding of the rules by which people live together in society," concludes historian Selma R. Williams.

Nothing escaped her attention. Though female and therefore a member of what she herself had labeled "that foolish sex," she knew enough about the political system in Massachusetts to be able to draw a comparison with that of Connecticut....Thus, she emerges as a political and economic feminist, whose demonstrated

Children attend a dame school. American girls typically received only a basic education.

independence and writing form a strong bridge from Puritanism to later Revolutionary-inspired agitation for equal rights and status. [102]

Women and the Vote

For the most part, it was not legislation or regulations that kept women out of politics but rather custom and convention. For example, many colonies did not explicitly bar women from voting; they simply outlined the property requirements and assumed that women would not meet such requirements. In fact, in some colonies, a few women of property, usually widows, did vote. Under the 1691 charter granted to Massachusetts, for example, women who held property could vote for all elective officers, as well as on the use and distribution of common land, improvements for the town, and new roads. Women landowners appeared on polling lists in Boston, Cambridge, Scituate, Weston, and Worcester. Women property owners were also on the voting rolls in a few places in Vermont and in Wetherfield and Windsor, Connecticut.

The number of women who cast votes was small, however. Even where female property owners were granted the right to vote, there is scant evidence that women took advantage of—or even knew about—this right. Historian Christopher Collier calls the cases of women voting in elections "extremely rare and . . . considered at the time to be freakish." [103]

Margaret Brent was probably the first woman to publicly insist on the right to vote. Brent and her sister Mary moved from England to Maryland in 1638, bringing nine settlers with them. The sisters set up manors (plantations of one thousand acres or more) and sent requests to England for more settlers. Margaret Brent proved to be an exceptional businesswoman and amassed a small fortune through trade in tobacco, indentured servants, and land. She also appeared in court several times in lawsuits against debtors and to protect her own interests. She acted on behalf of her brothers as well.

On his deathbed in 1647, Leonard Calvert, the governor of Maryland, appointed Thomas Greene as his successor as governor but entrusted his personal estate to Margaret Brent. "I make you my sole Exequtrix," he told her. "Take all, pay all." [104] With this appointment, Brent assumed responsibility for Calvert's assets—and his liabilities. Calvert's estate amounted to only about 110 pounds, not nearly enough to pay off his debts. But he had power of attorney for his brother, Lord Baltimore, and Margaret Brent got the court to agree to pass on this power to her.

The most pressing problem was paying mercenary soldiers who had been hired to quench a revolt that had temporarily driven Calvert from the governorship. The sol-

Not Fit for Intellectual Pursuits

The prevailing wisdom during the seventeenth century was that women's delicate nature made them unfit for reading, writing, or other intellectual pursuits, not to mention politics. John Winthrop, a well-respected Boston Puritan leader, wrote the following warning in 1645 to husbands who mistakenly believed that their wives could handle intellectual activity. This is reprinted in Kemp Battle's *Hearts of Fire*.

Mr. Hopkins, the governor of Hartford upon Connecticut, came to Boston, and brought his wife with him, (a godly young woman, and of special parts,) who was fallen into a sad infirmity, the loss of her understanding and reason, which had been growing upon her diverse years, by occasion of her giving herself wholly to reading and writing, and had written many books. Her husband, being very loving and tender of her, was loath to grieve her; but he saw his error, when it was too late. For if she had attended her household affairs, and such things as belong to women, and not gone out of her way and calling to meddle in such things as are proper for men, whose minds are stronger, she had kept her wits, and might have improved them usefully and honorably in the place God had set her. He brought her to Boston, and left her with her brother, one Mr. Yale, a merchant, to try what means might be had here for her. But no help could be had.

diers threatened to overthrow the new governor if they were not paid. Since Brent had the power of attorney for Lord Baltimore, she decided to sell some of Lord Baltimore's cattle to pay the soldiers.

Her most famous action, however, was to demand the vote. Actually, she claimed the right to two votes on the Maryland assembly, one as a property owner and another as executrix of the Calvert estate. When the governor refused, she left, saying that she "protested against all proceedings . . . unless she may be present and have [a] vote." [105]

Historians believe that Brent expected the Maryland assembly to deny her the vote and that she was trying to call attention to the urgency of the financial situation of Maryland. With the soldiers on the verge of mutiny, she did not have time to get Lord Baltimore's permission to sell some of his assets. The very day Maryland denied her the vote, however, she began to use her power of attorney to dispose of his property without his consent, giving a cow to a soldier. Margaret Brent handled affairs in Maryland so adeptly that she won the respect not only of the disgruntled soldiers

Widows and Politics

Women sometimes were prepared for politics because of their husbands' role. Elizabeth Turgis Blake, the wife of Governor Joseph Blake of South Carolina, is among the many women who used the intimate knowledge of politics gained through powerful male relations in an attempt to influence the governance of the colonies. Selma R. Williams writes that after Governor Blake died in 1700, Elizabeth "attempted to exert influence on such weighty matters as taxation and free speech." In a letter to the legislators in England she complained that the combination of heavy taxes and suppression of the right to protest would soon be "a fatal discouragement of the further and better settlement of this part of your Lordships' province."[107]

Just as taking on a deceased husband's responsibilities might require a woman to learn a "masculine" trade, so too might it require a woman to enter the public arena. Thus in 1768, Sarah Jenckes became the collector of rates and taxes when her husband died.

Widows were in a particularly precarious position. In some colonies, if a man died without a will, it was left to the magistrates to determine how to distribute his property. The judges often also assumed oversight of the widow's affairs. In New Haven, Connecticut, for example, judges supervised

A Quaker matron. Although most colonial men felt women to be intellectually unfit, Quakers believed in the equality of women—including their intelligence.

but of members of Parliament as well. When Lord Baltimore complained from England about her handling of the affairs in Maryland, the colonial legislative assembly backed her decision, saying, "without Mistress Brent, all would have gone to ruin."[106]

widows' payments to their children; in Massachusetts Bay, widows needed to get the magistrates' permission before they could sell any inherited real estate. Some women rebelled against such restrictions. In 1657, when the townsmen of Providence, Rhode Island, attempted to settle the estate of Nicholas Power, they reported in "puzzlement and frustration" that his widow Jane refused "to yeald obedience to the Law of the Colony." [108] Jane Power succeeded in resisting rule over her decisions and managed her property for over a decade, during which the Providence officials applauded her industry and her ability to increase her assets.

Women's Groups

Denied the right to vote or hold political office, many colonial women used their

---

Anne Bradstreet

Even while abiding the customs of the day, many women showed intellectual promise. As the daughter and wife of governors, Anne Bradstreet was exposed to political thought and was better educated than most of her female colleagues. She put her intellectual prowess to work writing poetry and in 1650 became the first American to publish a book of poetry.

Anne Dudley was born in 1613 in Northampton, England, and married Simon Bradstreet at the age of sixteen. Two years later, the Bradstreets and Dudleys embarked on the *Arabella,* members of the Puritan community that established godly community in the New World.

Anne Bradstreet was in many ways a typical Puritan goodwife. She became a devout member of the community, bearing and raising eight children, and most of her poetry reveals a woman who was satisfied with her lot as a woman. She wrote passionately about her love for her husband, tenderly about her children, even fondly of her household responsibilities. Some of her poems expressed a fear of childbirth and deep sorrow at the death of her children. Yet, some of her poems reveal that she recognized that women were worth more than men thought. The following excerpt is from a poem addressed to Queen Elizabeth, reprinted from Elisabeth Anthony Dexter's *Colonial Women of Affairs.*

Nay say, have women worth, or have they none?
Or had they some, but with our queen it's gone?
Nay masculines, you have thus taxed us long,
But she, though dead, will vindicate our wrong.
Let such as say our sex is void of reason
Know 'tis a slander now, but once was treason.

---

influence behind the scenes. They gathered together in meetings that, over time, took on a somewhat political tone. And in Charles Town, South Carolina, a doctor reported in 1707 that "the local women had a club that met weekly and were turning themselves into politicians."[109] Similar women's meetings grew up throughout the colonies. Most concentrated on nonpolitical issues, which might include caring for widows or poor families, but sometimes these meetings became covertly, if not overtly, political. One historian writes that the in-house meetings of the elite women in Manhattan were "centres of the petticoat government that . . . often controlled the affairs of the Colony."[110]

Women also took independent action. During Bacon's rebellion—a popular uprising in Virginia in the mid–seventeenth century—women provided food and shelter for Nathaniel Bacon and his followers as they fled from Virginia authorities. Some of these sympathizers had husbands among Bacon's troops. The wife of Anthony Haviland, for example, smuggled papers to the rebels at great risk to herself. Others were involved in the insurrection on their

Women in colonial America often met in homes like this one to discuss political and social issues.

own behalf. Virginia's Governor Berkeley called Sara Grendon a "great encourager and assister in the . . . horrid rebellion"[111] and exempted her from the pardon he gave to her fellow Charles City townspeople.

Educated women also used the pen as a weapon for (or against) various causes. During the French and Indian War, for example, tales of captives taken during Native American raids were sometimes used as propaganda to stir up emotion against the French. A 1756 advertisement in the *Boston Evening Post* tells of "A [woman's] Narrative . . . wherein it fully appears, that the Barbarities of the Indians is owing to the French, and chiefly their Priests."[112]

Mob Rule

Women certainly were aware of the politics of the day, because colonial America was a public place. Colonists often took to the streets to express their views. Popular decisions brought people out of their homes in celebration. The British victory in the French and Indian War in 1763, for example, caused week-long public celebrations in which the colonists toasted the king and the mother country.

Unpopular decisions were also causes for direct action, drawing crowds who sang, chanted, and cursed. Unpopular leaders were burned in effigy. Riots broke out. "While colonial America was by no means in a continual uproar," explains Stephanie Grauman Wolf, "the thinness of govern-

ment institutions suggests that a great many inhabitants were involved at some time in their lives in crowd action either as participants or observers. 'Legitimate' mob action . . . was an expression of communal political feelings that lacked an outlet within the framework of ordinary government."[113]

Women often played important roles in such events. Throughout the 1760s and 1770s, as mobs joined to protest British legislation, women regularly attended such events as the commemoration of the repeal of the Stamp Act and the hanging of British sympathizers in effigy. As a group of men crept onto a British vessel in Boston Harbor to throw British tea overboard, women lined the banks to show their support.

A Growing Sense of Patriotism

The growing sentiment against British rule made it difficult to ignore the political events of the day. Newspaper articles and broadsides declared the laws unjust and called on the colonists to oppose them. Women who perceived themselves as uninterested in politics were quickly caught up in political thought and conversation. Politics began to creep into women's thoughts in diaries and letters, even as women apologized for lapsing into a realm that was not their own. Sarah Jay interrupted her political musings in a letter to her family with an apology: "I've transgress'd the line that I proposed to observe in my correspondence by slipping into politicks, but my country and my friend possess so entirely my thoughts that you must not wonder if my pen runs beyond the dictates of prudence." [114]

Abigail Adams was among those who took a bold view of the events of the day. On November 12, 1775, she wrote to her husband John to encourage him to take action to separate from England:

> I could not join you today, in the petitions of our worthy pastor, for a reconciliation between our no-longer parent state, but tyrant state, and these colonies. Let us separate; they are unworthy to be our brethren. Let us renounce them; and instead of supplications as formerly, for their prosperity and happiness, let us beseech the Almighty to blast their counsels, and bring to nought all their devices. [115]

Mercy Otis Warren

Most women confined their political musings to private letters and conversations, but Bostonian Mercy Otis Warren took her ideas public. It was perhaps inevitable that Warren should become interested in politics. The Otises had a reputation as "troublemakers," writes Carol Berkin. "Many a New England Loyalist's diary or postwar memoirs held [Mercy's father and brother]

John Adams's wife, Abigail, supported the separation of the colonies from England.

entirely responsible for the Revolution." [116] As the wife of the Massachusetts legislator James Warren, Mercy Otis Warren had access to the inner circles of radical politics. Remarkably well educated for her day, Warren joined her husband and brother as they met with John and Samuel Adams and other patriots in their discussions of political events and strategy planning sessions held in the Warrens' home.

As the political crisis between Great Britain and its colonies escalated, Warren decided to put her writing talent to work for the colonial cause against Britain. During the early 1770s, her satirical prose and poems were published throughout the colonies. She also wrote several plays. *The Group,* published in 1775, satirized Massachusetts governor Thomas Hutchinson;

The Squabble of the Sea-Nymphs tells the story of the Boston Tea Party.

Warren appreciated the fact that she was moving beyond what was considered a woman's sphere and worried about whether this was appropriate. She published most of her political writing anonymously. Yet she was highly effective. Historian Berkin writes, "Because she had a genius for satire, a flair for drama, and a willingness to use both, she became the opposition's most effective shaper of popular opinion save perhaps for Samuel Adams." [117]

Boycotting British Goods

As England began to tighten its hold on the colonies, women increasingly saw themselves as active participants in the events of the day. As one woman wrote, "Tho a female I was born a patriot and cant help it If I would." [118]

And men needed women's participation. Recognizing the importance of a united front, the men leading the opposition to Britain's laws called upon women to help by boycotting British goods. In 1769 South Carolina legislator Christopher Gadsden spoke of the need to convince women to join the boycott: "I come here . . . to persuade our wives to give us our assistance, without which 'tis impossible to succeed. Only let their husbands point out the necessity of such conduct; convince them, that it is the only thing that can save them and their children, from distress, slavery, and disgrace; their affections will be, and cooperate with their reason." [119]

But women needed little encouragement to support the boycotts. In city after city, women banded together and pledged to boycott English products. To protest the mandate to buy tea only from England,

The Politics of Drinking Tea

The patriotic women who boycotted tea and European cloth were well aware of the political nature of their boycotts. Philadelphia resident Hana Griffits set the politics of tea to verse, calling on others to give up tea unless England repealed taxes on the colonies. The following poem is reprinted from Carol Berkin's *First Generations: Women in Colonial America.*

For the sake of Freedom's name
Since British Wisdom scorns repealing
Come, sacrifice to Patriot fame
And give up Tea, by way of healing
This done, within ourselves retreat.
The Industrious arts of life to follow
Let proud Nabobs storm and fret
They cannot force our lips to swallow.

some women organized anti-tea leagues that, encouraged "liberty tea," homemade brews from raspberry, sage, and other ingredients that could be found on American soil. Hundreds of Bostonian women took their private boycot public by affixing their names to a document binding themselves not to drink any tea until after the law was repealed. The document read: "We, the daughters of those patriots who have, and do now, appear for the public interest and in that principally regard their posterity—as such, do with pleasure engage with them in denying themselves the drinking of foreign tea, in hopes to frustrate a plan which tends to deprive a whole community of all that is valuable in life." [120] When the local magistrates granted a sick woman in Salem, Massachusetts, an exemption from the town's boycott on tea, she steadfastly refused, saying it was a matter of personal principle.

Cloth was another British commodity that the American rebels learned to live without. Even the wealthiest patriots were impelled to forsake their fine silk and satin garments for clothes made from coarser American cloth. "Indeed," concludes Carl Holliday, "it became a matter of genuine pride to many a patriotic dame that she could thus use the spinning wheel in behalf of her country." [121] Throughout the war, Martha Washington kept sixteen or more spinning wheels in constant operation at her luxurious home in Mount Vernon, Virginia.

Women sometimes took direct action to enforce the boycott on British goods. They ransacked stores that were owned by British sympathizers or that continued to sell British goods. They also dealt harshly with those who they believed unfairly

As American women organized boycotts against British goods such as silk and lace, dressing up like the woman shown here became unpatriotic.

Women of Colonial America

Abigail Adams

Abigail Smith Adams was born in 1744 in Weymouth, Massachusetts. The daughter of the Reverend William Smith, Weymouth's Congregational minister, Abigail had little formal education. Yet, even as a child, she had an atypically keen interest in history, literature, and politics.

She met John Adams, a twenty-five-year-old Massachusetts lawyer, at just fifteen, and the two married in 1764. During and after the American Revolution, Abigail and John Adams were separated for long periods of time, as John served as a delegate to Congress and a diplomat in Europe. They wrote regularly to one another, however, and their letters reveal much about their relationship and about the world in which they lived.

Insightful, witty, and intensely concerned with politics, Abigail Adams shared with John her opinions of the events of the day. She looked on to the growing resentment against British rule in the 1770s with enthusiasm, heartily supporting her husband's role in seeking independence. In her now-famous "Remember the Ladies" letter, Abigail proposed—perhaps tongue in cheek—that women would rebel if the new government did not secure for them the same freedoms sought for men. Abigail Adams also advocated the abolition of slavery and stressed the need for education for women, arguing that only educated women could provide their children with the character and skills needed to be leaders. Her own lack of formal schooling seemed not to be an impediment, however. Her husband continued to seek her guidance as vice president and president of the new nation. Seven years after Abigail's death in 1818, her oldest son, John Quincy Adams, became the sixth president of the United States.

drove up the prices on local goods. In 1777 twenty-two women, accompanied by two Continental army soldiers, confronted a Poughkeepsie, New York, merchant who was hoarding sugar. When the women broke into the merchant's home, he offered to sell the sugar at an inflated price, but the women declared they would have it on their own terms, loaded up as much sugar as they could carry, and left behind what they believed to be fair payment.

A year later, almost a hundred women confronted a wealthy Boston merchant suspected of hoarding coffee. Abigail Adams described the scene to her husband, John:

> A number of females, some say a hundred, some say more, assembled with a cart and trunks, marched down to the warehouse, and demanded the keys, which he refused to deliver. Upon which one of them seized him

by his neck and tossed him into the cart. . . . [Upon obtaining the keys, the women] opened the warehouse, hoisted out the coffee themselves, put it into the trunks and drove off. . . . A large concourse of men stood amazed, silent spectators of the whole transaction. [122]

Life in Wartime

The advent of the American Revolution expanded women's roles dramatically. In early 1774, as local militias prepared to fight the British, women mobilized for war. An eyewitness described the scene: "at every house Women and Children [were] making Cartridges, running Bullets, making Wallets, baking Biscuit, crying and bemoaning & at the same time animating their Husbands & Sons to fight for their liberties, tho not knowing whether they should ever see them again." [123]

Women joined together at spinning and sewing bees, where they not only turned out American thread and cloth but also made and mended the uniforms of the colonial troops. Girls and their mothers knitted socks for the troops. Women's organizations also held fund-raising campaigns and drives for metal goods that could be made into ammunition. Some women of modest means gave generously to the effort. "One New England woman," writes Carol Berkin, "eager to contribute metal for bullets, melted down not only her pewter tableware and her clockweights but all the nameplates from her family's tombstones." [124]

When war came, thousands of women followed their husbands to battle. Women served as cooks, bakers, laundresses, and nurses. Women carried water and ammunition. Mary Hays Ludwig, who became known as Molly Pitcher because she carried water to the American troops, took over her husband's position at a cannon when he suddenly collapsed during a 1778 battle in New Jersey. Throughout the rest of the battle, she loaded and fired the cannon. Other women donned men's clothing so that they would be able to enlist. The most famous of these women was Deborah Samson, who fought for two and a half years before a physician, while tending to an illness, discovered she was a woman.

Women also capitalized on the presumption that they were ignorant of politics to become successful spies. Some women listened in on conversations of the British troops as they did their laundry or sold them food. As Lydia Darragh innocently served meals to the British troops camped in Philadelphia, she listened carefully to their plans for a spring campaign. She then wrote up the strategy while it was still fresh in her mind, sewed the plans into the pockets of her coat, and smuggled the messages past unsuspecting British guards for delivery to George Washington. For

When her husband collapses, Molly Pitcher takes over his position at a cannon in the Battle of Monmouth. Thousands of women participated in the Revolutionary War.

months, fifteen-year-old Dicey Langston took careful note of the number, supplies, and morale of the British troops camped next to her father's farm and conveyed this information to nearby American forces.

The Loyalists

Of course, some women remained loyal to England, and they were no less involved. Loyalist women, like their patriot counterparts, took great risks to aid their side, serving as spies, saboteurs, and letter carriers for the English. Although the British army was much better equipped than the Continental army, women also supported their cause

financially. One Loyalist women's organization raised enough money to buy a ship and outfit it to fight against the Continental army.

The Dawn of a New Era

Americans planned a new government for themselves even as the Revolutionary War began. With the thoughts of equality and justice ringing in the air, women looked forward with hope to a new day, when they too might have new rights and new opportunities. When John Adams went to the Second Continental Congress in 1776, his wife Abigail wrote to him:

In the new Code of Laws which I suppose it will be necessary for you to make, I desire you would Remember the Ladies, and be more generous and favourable to them than your ancestors. Do not put such unlimited power into the hands of the Husbands. Remember all Men would be tyrants if they could. If perticular care and attention is not paid to the Ladies, we are determined to foment a Rebelion, and will not hold ourselves bound by any Laws in which we have no voice, or Representation. [125]

As the new country began to take its first steps, women believed that they would make, and were already making, progress. Judith Sargent Murray looked optimistically at the headway women were making in securing an education. "Female academies are everywhere establishing," she wrote in 1798. "I may be accused of enthusiasm; but such is my confidence in THE SEX that I expect to see our young women forming a new era in female history." [126]

Despite these great hopes and the contributions women had made, the achievement of independence failed to bring about a revolution in the roles and rights of women. American women remained outside the political mainstream. The property of wives remained under the control of their husbands. Women were still restricted from holding political office or voting.

In some ways, the lives of women had changed. During the decades-long struggle to forge a life in the wilderness and to break free of the tyranny of the mother country, women had learned much about their strengths and abilities, collectively and independently. But like their male colleagues, women continued to believe that their legitimate role was to care for their families. For many decades to come, the lives of early American women, like those of the colonists who preceded them, continued to revolve around home and hearth.

Notes

❦

Chapter 1: Women in Native American Communities

1. Quoted in Sara M. Evans, *Born for Liberty: A History of Women in America.* New York: Free Press Paperbacks, 1997, p. 14.
2. Quoted in Jane Kamensky, *The Colonial Mosaic: American Women, 1600–1760.* New York: Oxford University Press, 1995, p. 29.
3. Quoted in Selma R. Williams, *Demeter's Daughters: The Women Who Founded America, 1587–1787.* New York: Atheneum, 1976, p. 10.
4. Quoted in Time-Life Editors, *Realm of the Iroquois.* Alexandria, VA: Time-Life Books, 1992, p. 36.
5. Quoted in Time-Life Editors, *Realm of the Iroquois,* p. 37.
6. Quoted in Time-Life Editors, *Realm of the Iroquois,* p. 47.
7. Quoted in Evans, *Born for Liberty,* p. 11.
8. Kamensky, *The Colonial Mosaic,* p. 17.
9. Kamensky, *The Colonial Mosaic,* p. 17.
10. Quoted in Time-Life Editors, *The Woman's Way.* Alexandria, VA: Time-Life Books, 1995, p. 112.
11. Quoted in Laurel Thatcher Ulrich, *Good Wives: Image and Reality in the Lives of Women in Northern New England, 1650–1750.* New York: Vintage, 1991, p. 206.
12. Quoted in Williams, *Demeter's Daughters,* p. 161.
13. Quoted in June Namias, *White Captives: Gender and Ethnicity of the American Frontier.* Chapel Hill: University of North Carolina Press, 1993, p. 175.
14. Quoted in Williams, *Demeter's Daughters,* p. 168.
15. Quoted in Evans, *Born for Liberty,* p. 25.
16. Reader's Digest Editors, *Through Indian Eyes: The Untold Story of Native American Peoples.* Pleasantville, NY: Reader's Digest, 1995, p. 137.
17. Evans, *Born for Liberty,* p. 12.

Chapter 2: Colonial Women in the Home and Family

18. William Bradford, *Of Plymouth Plantation: The Pilgrims in America,* ed. Harvey Wish. New York: Paragon, 1962, p. 12.

19. Williams, *Demeter's Daughters,* pp. 50–51.

20. Kamensky, *The Colonial Mosaic,* p. 36.

21. Kamensky, *The Colonial Mosaic,* p. 36.

22. Quoted in Kamensky, *The Colonial Mosaic,* pp. 23–24.

23. Quoted in Williams, *Demeter's Daughters,* p. 33.

24. Eleanor Flexner and Ellen Fitzpatrick, *Century of Struggle: The Woman's Rights Movement in the United States.* Cambridge, MA: Belknap Press of Harvard University Press, 1996, p. 5.

25. Quoted in Williams, *Demeter's Daughters,* p. 52.

26. Quoted in Kamensky, *The Colonial Mosaic,* pp. 46–47.

27. Mary Beth Norton, *Founding Mothers and Fathers: Gendered Power and the Forming of American Society.* New York: Knopf, 1996, p. 223.

28. Carl Holliday, *Woman's Life in Colonial Days.* Williamstown, MA: Corner House, 1968, p. 108.

29. Holliday, *Woman's Life in Colonial Days,* p. 108.

30. Williams, *Demeter's Daughters,* p. 43.

31. Stephanie Grauman Wolf, *As Various as Their Land: The Everyday Lives of Eighteenth-Century Americans.* New York: HarperCollins, 1993, p. 95.

32. Wolf, *As Various as Their Land,* p. 96.

33. Quoted in Wolf, *As Various as Their Land,* p. 97.

34. Quoted in Williams, *Demeter's Daughters,* p. 20.

35. Holliday, *Woman's Life in Colonial Days,* p. 108.

36. Wolf, *As Various as Their Land,* p. 97.

37. Holliday, *Woman's Life in Colonial Days,* p. 113.

38. Quoted in Wolf, *As Various as Their Land,* p. 152.

39. Williams, *Demeter's Daughters,* p. 50.

40. Wolf, *As Various as Their Land,* p. 98.

41. Quoted in Holliday, *Woman's Life in Colonial Days,* p. 112.

Chapter 3: Servants and Slaves

42. Richard Hofstadter, *America at 1750: A Social Portrait.* New York: Vintage, 1973, p. 36.

43. Williams, *Demeter's Daughters,* pp. 57–58.

44. Hofstadter, *America at 1750,* pp. 43–44.

45. Hofstadter, *America at 1750,* p. 45.

46. Quoted in Kamensky, *The Colonial Mosaic,* p. 34.

47. Quoted in Doreen Rappaport, *American Women: Their Lives in Their Words.* New York: Thomas Y. Crowell, 1990, p. 11.

48. Quoted in Holliday, *Woman's Life in Colonial Days,* pp. 285–86.

49. Quoted in Flexner and Fitzpatrick, *Century of Struggle,* p. 17.

50. Carol Berkin, *First Generations: Women in Colonial America.* New York: Hill and Wang, 1996, p. 111.

51. Eugene D. Genovese, *Roll, Jordan, Roll: The World the Slaves Made.* New York: Vintage, 1976, p. 495.

52. Quoted in Genovese, *Roll, Jordan, Roll,* p. 499.

53. Berkin, *First Generations,* p. 121.

54. Quoted in Kamensky, *The Colonial Mosaic,* p. 42.

55. Quoted in Allen Weinstein, Frank Otto Gatell, and David Sarasohn, *American Negro Slavery: A Modern Reader.* 3rd ed. New York: Oxford University Press, 1979, p. 146.

56. Berkin, *First Generations,* p. 118.

57. Hofstadter, *America at 1750,* p. 93.

Chapter 4: Colonial Women in the Workforce

58. Wolf, *As Various as Their Land,* p. 185.

59. Quoted in Williams, *Demeter's Daughters,* p. 194.

60. Kamensky, *The Colonial Mosaic,* p. 65.

61. Berkin, *First Generations,* p. 80.

62. Ulrich, *Good Wives,* p. 39.

63. Quoted in Ulrich, *Good Wives,* p. 36.

64. Berkin, *First Generations,* pp. 30–31.

65. Quoted in Kamensky, *The Colonial Mosaic,* p. 138.

66. Wolf, *As Various as Their Land,* p. 97.

67. Evans, *Born for Liberty,* p. 36.

68. Elisabeth Anthony Dexter, *Colonial Women of Affairs, Before 1776.* Clifton, NJ: Augustus M. Kelley, 1972, p. 2.

69. Williams, *Demeter's Daughters,* p. 177.

70. Wolf, *As Various as Their Land,* pp. 200–201.

71. Quoted in Dexter, *Colonial Women of Affairs,* p. 59.

72. Quoted in Williams, *Demeter's Daughters,* p. 196.

73. Quoted in Dexter, *Colonial Women of Affairs,* p. 41.

74. Williams, *Demeter's Daughters,* p. 188.

75. Quoted in Wolf, *As Various as Their Land,* p. 102.

76. Quoted in Kamensky, *The Colonial Mosaic,* p. 132.

77. Quoted in Williams, *Demeter's Daughters,* p. 182.

78. Quoted in Williams, *Demeter's Daughters,* p. 185.

Chapter 5: Church and Community Leaders

79. John Winthrop, "A Modell of Christian Charity," written for the Massachusetts Bay Colony, 1630, Liberty Net. www.libertynet.org/ ~edcivic.winthrop.html.

80. Ulrich, *Good Wives,* p. 216.

81. Quoted in Williams, *Demeter's Daughters,* p. 124.

82. Ulrich, *Good Wives,* p. 217.

83. Quoted in Ulrich, *Good Wives,* p. 219.

84. Flexner and Fitzpatrick, *Century of Struggle,* p. 9.

85. Quoted in Kamensky, *The Colonial Mosaic,* p. 85.

86. Quoted in Williams, *Demeter's Daughters,* pp. 115–16.

87. Quoted in Williams, *Demeter's Daughters,* p. 116.

88. Quoted in Mary Beth Norton, *In the Devil's Snare: The Salem Witchcraft Crisis of 1692.* New York: Knopf, 2002, p. 22.

89. Norton, *In the Devil's Snare,* p. 4.

90. Quoted in Tim Sutter, "Salem Witchcraft," April 2003, Salem Witch Trials. www.salemwitch trials.com.

91. Quoted in Kamensky, *The Colonial Mosaic,* p. 91.

92. Berkin, *First Generations,* p. 92.

93. Berkin, *First Generations,* p. 92.

94. Williams, *Demeter's Daughters,* pp. 125–26.

95. Quoted in George Dewan, "A Dangerous 1600s' Woman," *Long Island: Our Story,* LI History. www.newsday.com/extras/lihistory /3/hs304a.htm.

96. Quoted in Williams, *Demeter's Daughters,* p. 130.

97. Quoted in Dexter, *Colonial Women of Affairs,* p. 149.

98. Quoted in Dexter, *Colonial Women of Affairs,* p. 150.

99. Holliday, *Woman's Life in Colonial Days,* p. 69.

Chapter 6: Taking a Stand: Colonial Women as Political Activists

100. Quoted in Linda K. Kerber, "Ourselves and Our Daughters Forever," in Marjorie Spruill Wheeler, ed., *One Woman, One Vote: Rediscovering the Woman Suffrage Movement.* Troutdale, OR: NewSage, 1995, p. 25.

101. Quoted in Flexner and Fitzpatrick, *Century of Struggle,* p. 16.

102. Williams, *Demeter's Daughters,* p. 210.

103. Christopher Collier, "The American People as Christian White Men of Property: Suffrage and Elections in Colonial and Early National America," in Donald W. Rogers, ed., *Voting and the Spirit of American Democracy: Essays on the History of Voting and Voting Rights in America.* Urbana: University of Illinois Press, 1992, p. 22.

104. Quoted in James A. Henretta et al., *America's History.* 3rd ed., 1997, Early America. www.earlyamerica. com/review/1998/brent.html.

105. Quoted in Lois Green Carr, "Margaret Brent," February 7, 2002, Maryland State Archives.

www.mdarchives.state.md.us/msa /speccol/sc3500/sc3520/002100/ 002177/html/mbrent2.html.

106. Quoted in Doris Weatherford, *A History of the American Suffragist Movement.* Santa Barbara, CA: ABC-CLIO, 1998, p. 6.

107. Quoted in Williams, *Demeter's Daughters,* p. 191.

108. Quoted in Norton, *Founding Mothers and Fathers,* p. 148.

109. Quoted in Williams, *Demeter's Daughters,* p. 130.

110. Weatherford, *A History of the American Suffragist Movement,* pp. 5–6.

111. Quoted in Kamensky, *The Colonial Mosaic,* p. 110.

112. Quoted in Dexter, *Colonial Women of Affairs,* p. 138.

113. Wolf, *As Various as Their Land,* p. 254.

114. Quoted in Evans, *Born for Liberty,* p. 48.

115. Quoted in Kemp Battle, ed., *Hearts of Fire: Great Women of American Lore and Legend.* New York: Random House, 1997, p. 321.

116. Berkin, *First Generations,* p. 172.

117. Berkin, *First Generations,* p. 172.

118. Quoted in Evans, *Born for Liberty,* p. 48.

119. Quoted in Berkin, *First Generations,* p. 173.

120. Quoted in Flexner and Fitzpatrick, *Century of Struggle,* p. 12.

121. Quoted in Holliday, *Woman's Life in Colonial Days,* p. 111.

122. Quoted in Flexner and Fitzpatrick, *Century of Struggle,* pp. 12–13.

123. Quoted in Berkin, *First Generations,* pp. 178–79.

124. Berkin, *First Generations,* p. 180.

125. Quoted in Kerber, "Ourselves and Our Daughters Forever," in Wheeler, *One Woman, One Vote,* p. 24.

126. Quoted in Flexner and Fitzpatrick, *Century of Struggle,* p. 15.

For Further Reading

Books

Natalie S. Bober, *Abigail Adams: Witness to Revolution.* New York: Athenaeum, 1995. This biography of Abigail Adams focuses on her role prior to the American Revolution.

Beth Clark, ed., *Anne Hutchinson: Religious Leader.* Philadelphia: Chelsea House, 2000. At a time when women were expected to be subservient, Anne Hutchinson spoke her mind and shared her religious views. This suspenseful account of this daring woman highlights the theological and "feminist" issues that caused Hutchinson's banishment and excommunication.

Jacob Ernest Cooke and Milton M. Klein, eds., *North America in Colonial Times: An Encyclopedia for Students.* New York: Charles Scribner's Sons, 1998. This four-volume set covers the thirteen colonies that became the United States, as well as the colonization of Canadian and Spanish settlements in North America. The alphabetical arrangement, cross-references, time lines, and sidebars make it a highly useful and engaging reference source for students.

Deborah Crawford, *Four Women in a Violent Time: Anne Hutchinson (1591–1643); Mary Dyer (1591?–1660); Lady Deborah Moody (1600–1659); Penelope Stout (1622–1732).* New York: Crown, 1970. This narrative, which tells the stories of four leading ladies of the colonial era and brings them together in the historical context in which they lived, makes for highly informative and fun reading.

Jean Fritz, *The Double Life of Pocahontas.* New York: Puffin, 1987. This lively in-depth account of the life and times of this most famous Native American woman is told with a true storyteller's flair.

Mary Rodd Furbee, *Outrageous Women of Colonial America.* New York: John Wiley & Sons, 2001. This easy-to-read biography tells the stories of a few particularly daring and entrepreneurial colonial American women.

Cheryl Harness, *Remember the Ladies: 100 Great American Women.* New York: HarperCollins, 2001. This broad overview of notable American women includes biographies of several women who lived during the colonial period.

James Haskins and Kathleen Benson, *Building a New Land: African Americans in Colonial America.* New York: HarperCollins, 2001. A chronicle of the lives of slaves and their effect on colonial America from the 1600s to the American Revolution. Discusses how slaves resisted oppression and how they struggled to maintain the traditions of their rich African culture through music, dance, and storytelling.

Judith Head, *America's Daughters: 400 Years of American Women.* Los Angeles: Perspective, 1999. Two-page biographies of more than fifty women, organized by centuries beginning with the 1600s. Includes overviews of women's work and women's place; groups of women (such as Native American women, indentured women, slaves, or revolutionary women); and specific women who played a key role in the development of the nation. The result is an easy-to-follow, highly readable account of the lives of well-known and lesser-known women who made a difference.

Sarah Howarth, *Colonial People.* Brookfield, CT: Millbrook, 1994. An easy-to-read account of life and lives in colonial America.

Catherine Iannone, *Pocahontas.* New York: Chelsea House, 1996. A factual biographical account of the Powhatan princess. Includes original drawings, paintings, and quotes from primary sources.

Johanna Johnston, *They Led the Way: 14 American Women.* New York: Scholastic Paperbacks, 1992. The series of short biographies includes the stories of Anne Hutchinson, Anne Bradstreet, Deborah Moody, Phillis Wheatley, and Abigail Adams, as well as later leading female Americans.

Louise Chipley Slavicek, *Women of the Revolutionary War.* San Diego: Lucent, 2002. The story of the women of the American Revolution and the many roles they played in bringing about independence from England.

Carter Smith, ed., *Daily Life: A Sourcebook on Colonial America.* Brookfield, CT: Millbrook, 1991. Part of a series that illustrates major events through a wide variety of materials, including engravings, photographs, and excerpts from primary sources, this book focuses on the day-to-day life of colonial Americans.

Time-Life Editors, *Realm of the Iroquois.* Alexandria, VA: Time-Life Books, 1992. This easy-to-read account of the history and life of the Iroquois nations includes lots of photographs, maps, and artifacts.

John F. Warner, *Colonial American Home Life.* New York: Franklin Watts, 1993. An easy-to-read and well-illustrated account of how the people who settled the New World lived.

Websites

Alexander Street Press: North American Women's Letters and Diaries (www.alexanderstreet2.com/NWLDLive). Produced in collaboration with the University of Chicago, this site includes women's diaries and correspondence from the colonial era to the present. The site describes its completed collection as the largest ever assembled online, bringing the personal experiences of hundreds of women to researchers, students, and general readers.

American Women's History: A Research Guide for Colonial America (www.mtsu.edu/~kmiddlet/history/women/wh-colonial.html). This website lists references and resources, both in print and online, for further research on colonial America.

National Women's History Project (www.nwhp.org). The mission of the National Women's History Project is to recognize and celebrate the diverse and historic accomplishments of women by providing information and educational materials and programs. The website includes biographies of famous women and links to other websites.

University of Colorado, Colonial American History (www.uccs.edu history/index/colonial.html.). Sponsored by the University of Colorado, Colorado Springs, History Department, this website provides a list of links devoted to general resources, biographies, politics, and specific colonies.

Women's History (womenshistory.about.com). This website offers an encyclopedia of easily accessed and well-organized information on all aspects of women's history.

Works Consulted

Books

Kemp Battle, ed., *Hearts of Fire: Great Women of American Lore and Legend.* New York: Random House, 1997. This collection of excerpts by and about American folk heroines and other female leaders from all walks of life includes several articles of interest to those studying women of colonial America.

Carol Berkin, *First Generations: Women in Colonial America.* New York: Hill and Wang, 1996. A scholarly portrait of women in the variety of circumstances in which they lived and worked in colonial America and the many, varied roles they played.

William Bradford, *Of Plymouth Plantation: The Pilgrims in America.* Ed. Harvey Wish. New York: Paragon, 1962. This firsthand account of the Pilgrims' experience as they crossed the Atlantic Ocean and settled in Plymouth, Massachusetts, provides a glimpse of the many obstacles they faced and their struggles to forge a life in the wilderness.

Elisabeth Anthony Dexter, *Colonial Women of Affairs, Before 1776.* Clifton, NJ: Augustus M. Kelley, 1972. Originally written in 1924, this remains the most comprehensive account of colonial women's various occupations.

Sara M. Evans, *Born for Liberty: A History of Women in America.* New York: Free Press Paperbacks, 1997. This comprehensive history of women in America includes chapters on Native American women, the first white settlers, and women's roles in the American Revolution.

Eleanor Flexner and Ellen Fitzpatrick, *Century of Struggle: The Woman's Rights Movement in the United States.* Cambridge, MA: Belknap Press of Harvard University Press, 1996. This historical account of the woman's rights movement begins with a description of the roles women of various classes and regions played as they settled in the colonies of the New World.

Eugene D. Genovese, *Roll, Jordan, Roll: The World the Slaves Made.* New York: Vintage, 1976. This comprehensive and detailed analysis of American slavery emphasizes the perspectives of African slaves and their owners.

Richard Hofstadter, *America at 1750: A Social Portrait.* New York: Vintage,

1973. This colorful portrait of life in America in the mid–eighteenth century includes descriptions of the lives of men and women in all regions and of all social classes.

Carl Holliday, *Woman's Life in Colonial Days*. Williamstown, MA: Corner House, 1968. Written in 1922, this work makes extensive use of diaries, letters, and other contemporary sources to portray the everyday life of women in colonial America.

Jane Kamensky, *The Colonial Mosaic: American Women, 1600–1760*. Young Oxford History of Women in the United States Series. New York: Oxford University Press, 1995. This book makes extensive use of primary sources and rich details for an accessible history of the public and private lives of American women.

Kenneth Lockridge, *A New England Town: The First Hundred Years*. New York: W. W. Norton, 1970. This book tells the story of the town of Deadham, Massachusetts, from its founding in 1636 until the middle of the eighteenth century.

Richard Middleton, *Colonial America: A History, 1585–1776*. 2nd ed. Cambridge, MA: Blackwell, 1996. With chapters devoted to family life and women, this comprehensive analysis of the principal events and developments of colonial America includes ample discussion of social history and the status and roles of women.

June Namias, *White Captives: Gender and Ethnicity of the American Frontier*. Chapel Hill: University of North Carolina Press, 1993. This book tells the stories of American colonists who were captured by Native Americans. Their varied experiences reveal much about the complex relationships between Native Americans and colonists in the New World. Also discusses the role that gender played in the experiences of captives.

Mary Beth Norton, *Founding Mothers and Fathers: Gendered Power and the Forming of American Society*. New York: Knopf, 1996. An exploration of the distribution of power and the roles of men and women in seventeenth-century colonial America.

———, *In the Devil's Snare: The Salem Witchcraft Crisis of 1692*. New York: Knopf, 2002. This fresh look at the Salem witchcraft trials gives added emphasis to the role played by the ongoing conflict with Native Americans on the Maine frontier.

———, *Liberty's Daughters: The Revolutionary Experience of American Women, 1750–1800*. Boston: Little, Brown, 1980. A comprehensive account of the varied experiences of women living in the British colonies just prior to and during the American Revolution.

Doreen Rappaport, *American Women: Their Lives in Their Words.* New York: Thomas Y. Crowell, 1990. This book explores the roles of women in various periods of American history and, through excerpts from letters, diaries, speeches, and other writings, gives voice to real women of America.

Reader's Digest Editors, *Through Indian Eyes: The Untold Story of Native American Peoples.* Pleasantville, NY: Reader's Digest, 1995. This history of America is told from the viewpoint of Native Americans and makes ample use of illustrations and of quotations from native people, past and present.

Jerome R. Reich, *Colonial America.* 5th ed. Upper Saddle River, NJ: Prentice-Hall, 2001. A comprehensive account of the political, economic, social, and cultural life of colonial America, giving special attention to the roles of groups sometimes overlooked, such as Native Americans, African Americans, and women.

Donald W. Rogers, ed., *Voting and the Spirit of American Democracy: Essays on the History of Voting and Voting Rights in America.* Urbana: University of Illinois Press, 1992. Written by leading historians and political scientists, this collection of essays traces the history of voting in America from the colonial period to the present.

Time-Life Editors, *The Woman's Way.* Alexandria, VA: Time-Life Books, 1995. A title in the American Indians Series, this beautifully illustrated and lively book tells of the lives and work of Native American women.

Edwin Tunis, *Colonial Living.* New York: Thomas Y. Crowell, 1957. Through descriptions and illustrations, this book gives a glimpse of the housing, tools, and everyday items used by colonial men and women.

Laurel Thatcher Ulrich, *Good Wives: Image and Reality in the Lives of Women in Northern New England, 1650–1750.* New York: Vintage, 1991. This well-researched and detailed account of the lives of women in northern New England provides a lively account of the burdens, progress, and power of the typical colonial housewife.

Doris Weatherford, *A History of the American Suffragist Movement.* Santa Barbara, CA: ABC-CLIO, 1998. A lively and readable history of the woman suffrage movement in America that traces its roots to colonial America.

Allen Weinstein, Frank Otto Gatell, and David Sarasohn, *American Negro Slavery: A Modern Reader.* 3rd ed. New York: Oxford University Press, 1979. Scholarly essays cover various aspects of American slavery, including its effect on gender roles of both African American slaves and the whites who owned them.

Marjorie Spruill Wheeler, ed., *One Woman, One Vote: Rediscovering the Woman Suffrage Movement*. Troutdale, OR: NewSage, 1995. This companion to the PBS special of the same name includes essays by notable historians and scholars addressing various aspects of the woman suffrage movement and the status of women in general.

Selma R. Williams, *Demeter's Daughters: The Women Who Founded America, 1587–1787*. New York: Atheneum, 1976. An account of the contributions women made to the survival of those who settled in the New World and to the success of the British colonies.

Stephanie Grauman Wolf, *As Various as Their Land: The Everyday Lives of Eighteenth-Century Americans*. New York: HarperCollins, 1993. This well-researched popular history gives a detailed account of the richly diverse experiences of eighteenth-century women in colonial America.

Internet Sources

Ann Baker, "Margaret Brent," 1977, Maryland State Archives, www.md archives.state.md.us/msa/speccol/sc350 0/sc3520/002100/002177/html/brochure.html.

Lois Green Carr, "Margaret Brent," February 7, 2002, Maryland State Archives. www.mdarchives.state.md.us/msa/speccol/sc3500/sc3520/002100/002177/html/mbrent2.html.

George Dewan, "A Dangerous 1600s' Woman," *Long Island: Our Story*, LI History. www.newsday.com/extras/lihistory/3/hs304a.htm.

James A. Henretta et al., *America's History*. 3rd ed., 1997, Early America. www.early america.com/review/1998/brent.html.

Susan McCulley and Jen Loux, "Bacon's Rebellion," March 21, 2002, National Park Service. www.nps.gov/colo/Jthanout/BacRebel.html.

National Geographic Interactive, "Salem Witchcraft Hysteria," 1997, National Geographic Society. www.national geographic.com/features/97.

"The Salem Witch Trials of 1692," in *The Colonial Gazette*, 2000, Interactive Communications. www.mayflower families.com/enquirer/salem_witch_trials.htm.

Tim Sutter, "Salem Witchcraft," April 2003, Salem Witch Trials. www.salem witchtrials.com.

John Winthrop, "A Modell of Christian Charity," written for the Massachusetts Bay Colony, 1630, Liberty Net. www.libertynet.org/~edcivic/winthrop.html.

Index

Abenaki, 19, 20
Adams, Abigail Smith, 88, 91, 93–94
Adams, John, 80, 88, 91, 93–94
Adams, John Quincy, 91
Adams, Samuel, 88, 89
Algonquian, 8
  crops and, 9–10
  food gathering and, 9–10
  Pocahontas and, 13–14
America at 1750 (Hofstadter), 52
American Revolution, 92–93
Arabella, 85
As Various as Their Land (Wolf), 62
Axtell, Rebecca, 65

Bacon, Nathaniel, 86
Bacon's rebellion, 86
Baltimore, Lord, 82–84
Battle, Kemp, 31, 83
Belknap, Ruth, 34
Beloved Woman, 12–13, 16–17
Berkin, Carol, 18, 45, 52, 55, 56, 75, 88–89, 92
Blaikley, Catherine, 60
Blake, Elizabeth Turgis, 84
Blake, Joseph, 84
boarding schools, 59
Born for Liberty (Evans), 20, 64
Boston Evening Post (newspaper), 87
Boston Tea Party, 86, 89–90
Bourdet, Mrs. Samuel, 63
boycott, on British goods
  cloth and, 90
  enforcement of, 90–92
  support of, 89–90
  tea and, 89–90
  Boylston, Sarah, 63

Bradford, William, 24
Bradstreet, Anne, 85
Brent, Margaret, 63–64, 82–84
businesswomen, 55–57

Cahell, Mary, 63
Calvert, Leonard, 82–83
Campanella, Thomas J., 77–78
candle making, 33
Carter, Landon, 50
Catholic missionaries, 78
Century of Struggle (Flexner and Fitzpatrick), 48
Champlain, Samuel de, 11
Chebacco, Massachusetts, 69–70
Cherokee, 12, 16–17, 18
childbirth, 28
children, 28
Chippewa, 12
chores, 24, 28–30
church, 69–72
"civil death," 6
Clark, Mrs., 57
clothing, 31–33
Cockacoeske (Queen Anne), 17
Colden, Jane, 66
Collier, Christopher, 82
Colonial American Life (Warner), 32
Colonial Mosaic: American Women, The (Kamensky), 14, 34
Colonial Women of Affairs (Dexter), 62, 85
cooking, 29–32
Cooper, Mary, 27
Cooper, Susannah, 66
crafts, 60
Cree, 12–13
Crowley, Mary, 61

dame schools, 7, 58
Darragh, Lydia, 92
Demeter's Daughters (Selma R. Williams), 23
De Vries, Peter, 54
Dexter, Elisabeth Anthony, 57, 62, 85
Digges, Elizabeth, 65
disease, 33, 38, 40
Douglas, Catherine, 40
Duston, Hannah, 21
Dutch colonists, 54
Dyer, Mary, 77

Easty, Mary, 74–75
Eliot, Anne Mountford, 60
Evans, Sara M., 20, 23, 57

feme sole. See unmarried women
First Generations: Women in Colonial America (Berkin), 18, 89
Fitzpatrick, Ellen, 26–27, 48
Flexner, Eleanor, 26–27, 48
Founding Mothers and Fathers (Norton), 58, 73
Fowler, William, 22
Franklin, Benjamin, 56, 58
Franklin, Deborah Read, 56
French and Indian War, 17, 60, 87
Friends of American Manufacturers, 62
fur trading, 10–11, 17

Gadsden, Christopher, 89
Gardener's Calendar, The (Logan), 65
Gazette (newspaper), 61
Giton, Judith, 27
Good, Sarah, 72–73
Goose, Mrs., 61–62
gossip, 73
Grafton, Hannah, 62
Grant, Ann, 23
Gravesend, Long Island, 77–78
Great Lakes tribes, 10–11, 17
Greene, Thomas, 82
Grendon, Sara, 87

Griffits, Hana, 89
Group, The (play), 88
Guyart, Mary, 78

Hammon, Elizabeth, 20
Hardenbroek, Margaret, 54–55
Haviland, Mrs. Anthony, 86
Hearts of Fire (Battle), 31, 83
Heck, Barbara Ruckle, 78–79
Hewlett, Mistress, 63
hoecake, 29–30
Hofstadter, Richard, 52
Holliday, Carl, 28, 29, 33, 34, 79, 90
Holy Experiment, 75
Holyoke, Mary, 36
Hopkins, Elizabeth, 25
Huron Women, 11
Hutchinson, Anne Marbury, 70–72, 77
Hutchinson, Thomas, 88–89

indentured servants
  disease and, 38, 40
  hardships of, 37–40
  illegitimate children of, 40–42
  legal protection and, 43
  living conditions of, 39–40
  marriage and, 28, 40
  punishment of, 41–42, 49–50
  purchase of, 39
  sexual activity among, 40–41, 43
  terms of, 37
Indian scalps, 21
indigo, 65
innovations, 65–66
Iroquois, 8–9
  community leadership, 12
  food gathering, 9–10

Jamestown, Virginia
  founding of, 6
  Pocahontas and, 13–15
  shortage of wives and, 25

Jay, Sarah, 87–88
Jemison, Mary, 11, 20
Jenckes, Sarah, 84
Jewell, Sarah, 61
Johnson, Edward, 11
Johnston, Henrietta, 60
Jones, Anna, 61

Kamensky, Jane, 14, 15, 24
King, Elizabeth, 60
King George's War, 17
King Philip's War, 19, 20
King William's War, 17
Knight, Sarah, 58, 81

Lafitau, Joseph-François, 12
land inheritance, 64–65
Landscape Journal, 77–78
Langston, Dicey, 93
laws
  assets and, 55
  contracts and, 66
  land ownership and, 64
  religious, 67
  restrictions on women and, 53
Lennardson, Samuel, 21
Levine, Lawrence W., 51
Logan, Martha, 65
Long Island revolt, 50
Louisiana revolt, 50
Loyalists, 93
Ludwig, Mary Hays, 92
lye, 33

marriage, 11–13
Massachusetts Bay Colony, 67–68, 85
Masters, Sibylla, 66
Mather, Cotton, 19
Mather, Samuel, 58
matrilineal system, 11
Mayflower (ship), 25, 26

meals, 29
medicines, 31
Metacomet, 18
Middle Passage, 43
midwives, 59–60
mob uproars, 87
Montour, Madame, 15
Moody, Lady Deborah, 77–78
Murray, Elizabeth, 62
Murray, Judith, 80
Murray, Judith Sargent, 94
Musgrove, John, 16
Musgrove, Mary (Cousaponokesa), 16
Muskogean, 8

Nanapashemet, 17
*Narrative of the Captivity and Restoration of Mrs.
  Mary Rowlandson, The* (Rowlandson), 19
Native American women
  crops and, 8–9
  farming and, 20
  household duties of, 10
  marriage and, 11
  political roles of, 12–13
  as translators, 13
  travel and, 9
  war and, 18–21
Naumkeag, 17
Neff, Mary, 21
New England tribes, 17
New York City revolt, 50
nomadic tribes, 10
Norton, Mary Beth, 28, 58, 73
Nuthead, Dinah, 61

obedience, 28
occupations
  botany, 66
  crafts and, 60
  in male-dominated fields, 60–61
  medical, 60
  merchants, 61–63
  midwifery, 59–60

photography, 60
printing, 61
teaching, 58–59
textile companies, 62
Ogelthorp, James, 16
Ojibwa, 12

Parris, Reverend Samual, 72
Penn, William, 75
Pennsylvania Magazine, 44
Peters, John, 44
Philips, Elizabeth, 59–60
Philipsen, Frederick, 55
Phips, Governor, 75
Pinckney, Charles, 65
Pinckney, Eliza Lucas, 65
Pitcher, Molly. *See* Ludwig, Mary Hays
plantations, 35, 64–65
"Pleasures of a Country Life, The" (Belknap), 43
Plymouth, Massachusetts, 25
Pocahontas, 13–15
Poems on Various Subjects, Religious and Moral
   (Phillis Wheatley), 44
politics
   British resentment and, 87–91
   expression in, 87
   petition to be heard and, 64
   rights in, 80–81
   taxes and, 84
   voting and, 82–84
   widows and, 84–85
   women's groups and, 86–87
Powel, Elizabeth, 63
Powel, Samuel, 63
Power, Jane, 85
Power, Nicholas, 85
Powhatan (chief), 13–15, 17
Powhatan Confederacy, 17
Puritans, 67
   Anne Hutchinson and, 70–72
   Arabella and, 85
   colonies and, 25

laws and, 67–68
voting and, 82–84
witchcraft and, 72
women's roles and, 68, 70–71

Quakers, 67
   church and, 75
   leaders of, 77–78
   missionaries and, 76–77
Queen Anne's War, 17

Rebecca. *See* Pocahontas
religion
   denominations of, 78–79
   Puritan, 67–68
   Quaker, 75–78
Richard, John, 78
Roanoke, 15
Roberts, Mary, 60
Rolfe, John, 13–15
Rowlandson, Mary, 19
Russell, Elizabeth, 61

Salem witch trials, 72–74
Salisbery, Mary, 59
Salmon, Mary, 60
Samson, Deborah, 92
Sandys, Edwin, 25
Saugus, 17
Seneca, 11
shelters, Native American, 8, 12
she-merchants, 61–63
Shuyler, Cornelia, 63
Siouan, 8
slavery
   children and, 46
   Christian values and, 52
   culture development and, 51–52
   females and, 42
      as fieldworkers, 45
      as household slaves, 46
      status of, 48

labor of, 45–46
laws regulating, 43
marriage and, 47
motherhood and, 47–48
Phillis Wheatley and, 44, 45
population of, 43
revolts and, 50
runaways and, 49–50
slave quarters and, 46
slave ships and, 44–45
"Slave Songs and Slave Conscious" (Levine), 51
Smith, John, 13–15
Smith, Mary, 22
Smith, William, 91
soap making, 33
social contact
  "bees" and, 34
  childbirth and, 28
  church and, 68
  isolation from, 34
  religion and, 67
  trading networks and, 33–34
Squabble of the Sea Nymph, The (play), 89
Squaw Sachem of Massachusetts, 17
Starbuck, Mary Coffin, 78
Stockford, Goody, 20
Swarton, Hannah, 19

Taney, Mary, 78
teaching, 58–60
Thomas, Martha, 76
thread, spinning of, 31–32
Timothy, Elizabeth, 61
Tituba, 72–73
trade networks, 33–34

Ulrich, Laurel Thatcher, 55, 68, 69
unmarried women
  as businesswomen, 57, 59
  as land merchants, 63–64

workforce and, 53
see also widows

Varnod, Widow, 59
voting, 82–84

Ward, Bryant, 16
Ward, Nancy (Nanye'hi), 16–17
Warner, John F., 32
Warren, James, 88
Warren, Mercy Otis, 88–89
Washington, George, 44, 92
Washington, Martha, 35, 90
wealth, 36
Weekly Journal (newspaper), 64
Wetamo, 18
Wheaten, Sarah Haggar, 59
Wheatley, John, 44
Wheatley, Phillis, 44, 45
Wheatley, Susannah, 44
white encroachment, 16–17, 18
Whitefield, George, 44
Whitmore, Mrs. Thomas, 60
widows
  church and, 68
  income of, 57
  politics and, 84–85
  see also unmarried women
Williams, John, 20–21
Williams, Selma R., 23, 24, 29, 34, 77, 81, 84
Winnisimmit, 17
Winthrop, John, 70, 71–72, 83
Winthrop, Margaret, 72
witchcraft, 72–75
Wolf, Stephanie Grauman, 31, 33, 35, 53, 56, 60, 87
Woman's Life in Colonial Days (Holliday), 29
Wright, Susanna, 60

Zenger, Anna, 61
Zenger, John Peter, 61, 64

Picture Credits

About the Author

Lydia Bjornlund is a private consultant and freelance writer, focusing primarily on issues related to civic education, government, and training. This is her sixth book for Lucent Books.

Ms. Bjornlund holds a master's degree in education from Harvard University and a bachelor's degree from Williams College, where she majored in American studies. She lives in Oakton, Virginia, with her husband, Gerry Hoetmer, and their twins, Jake and Sophia.